French Bulldog Coloring Book

This Coloring book belongs to:

_____

Copyright © 2017 Adult Coloring Books

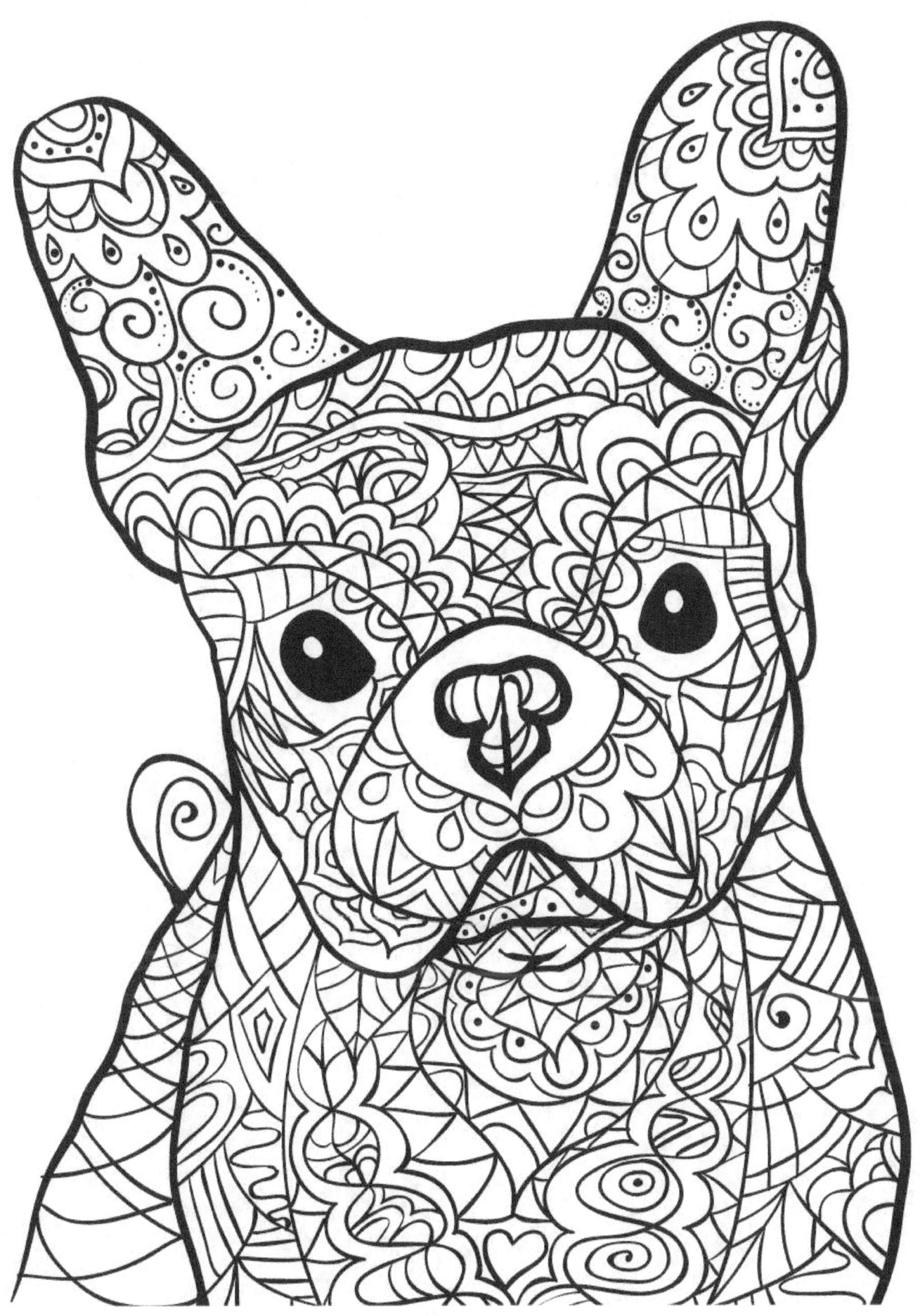

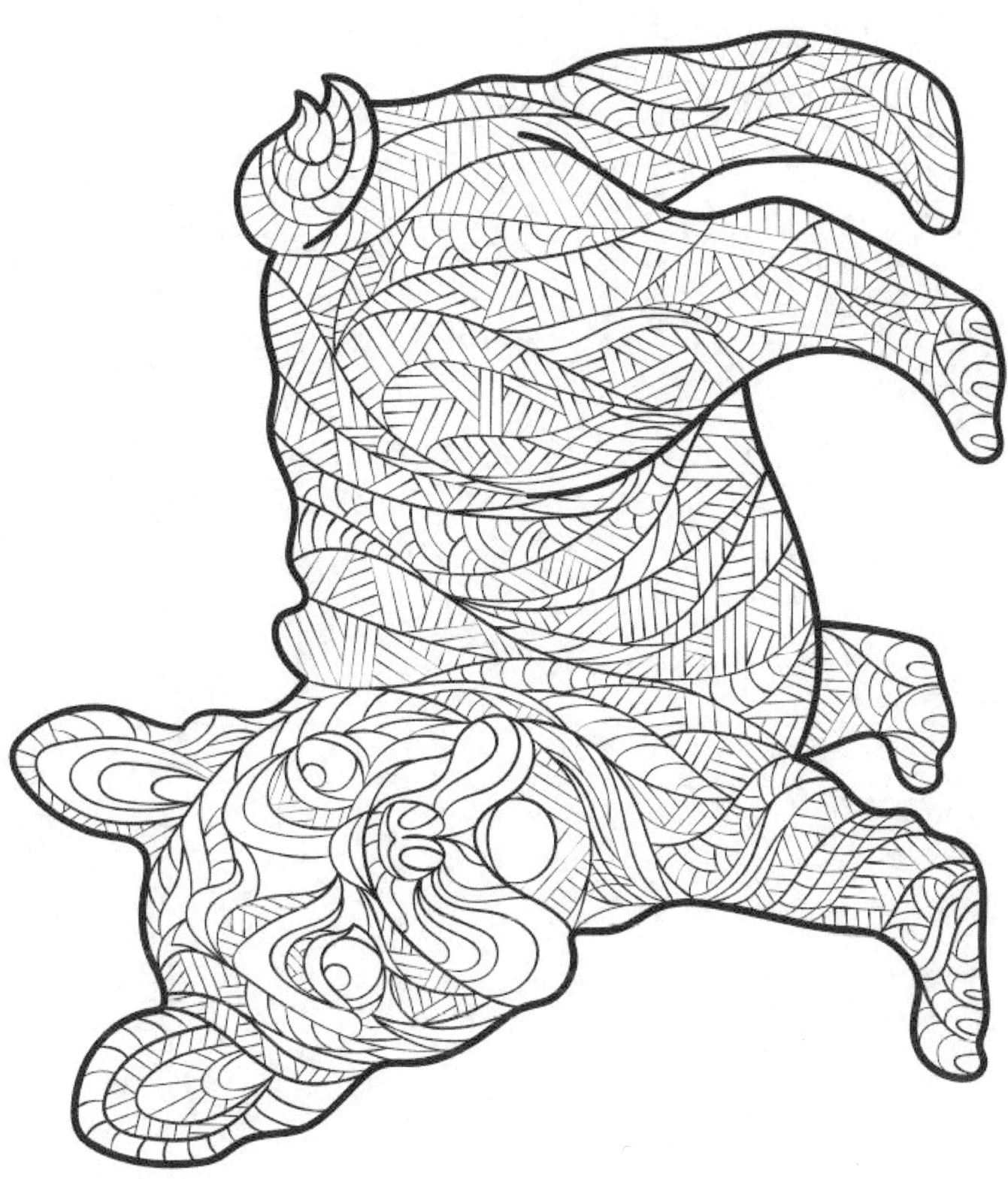

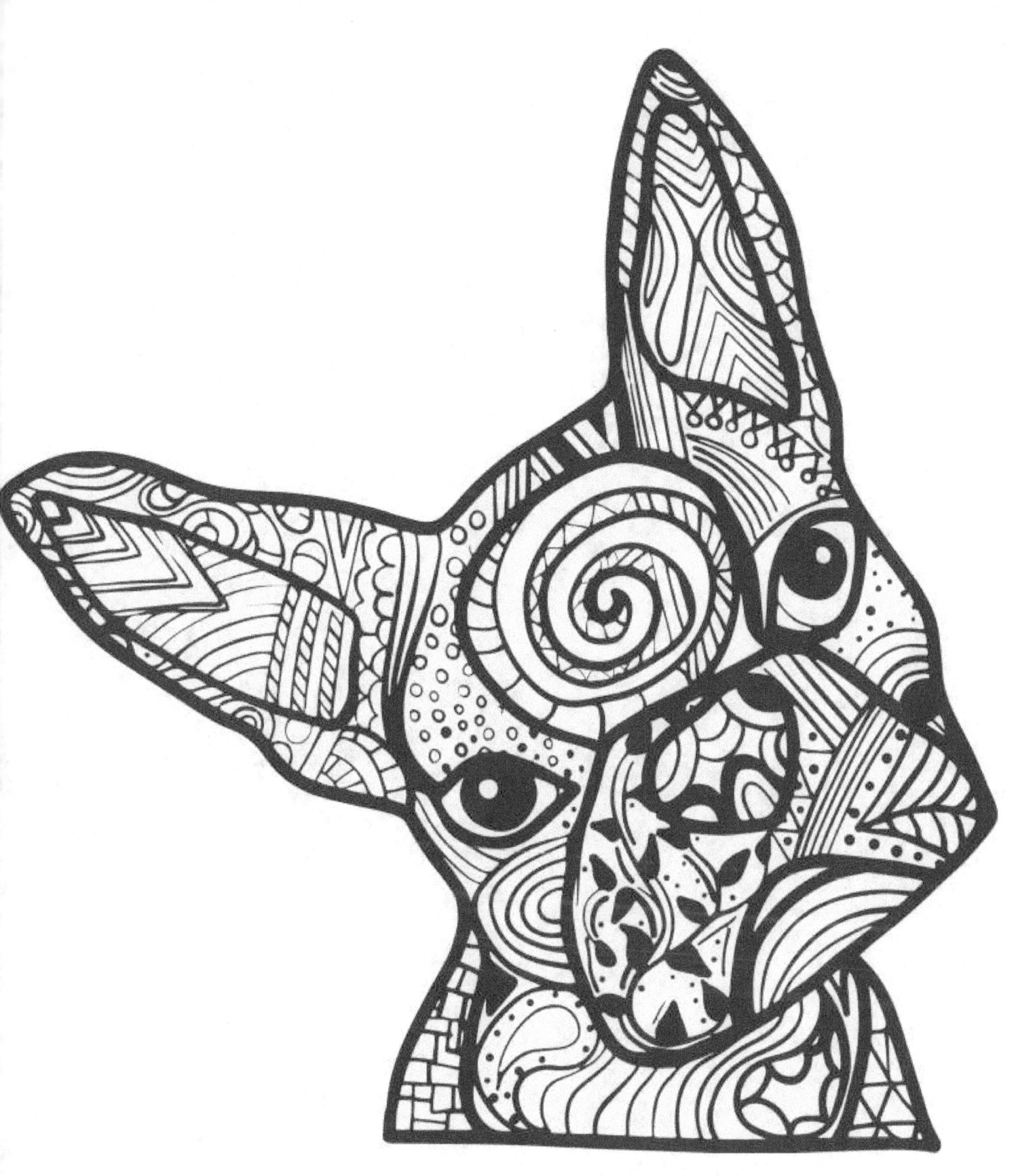

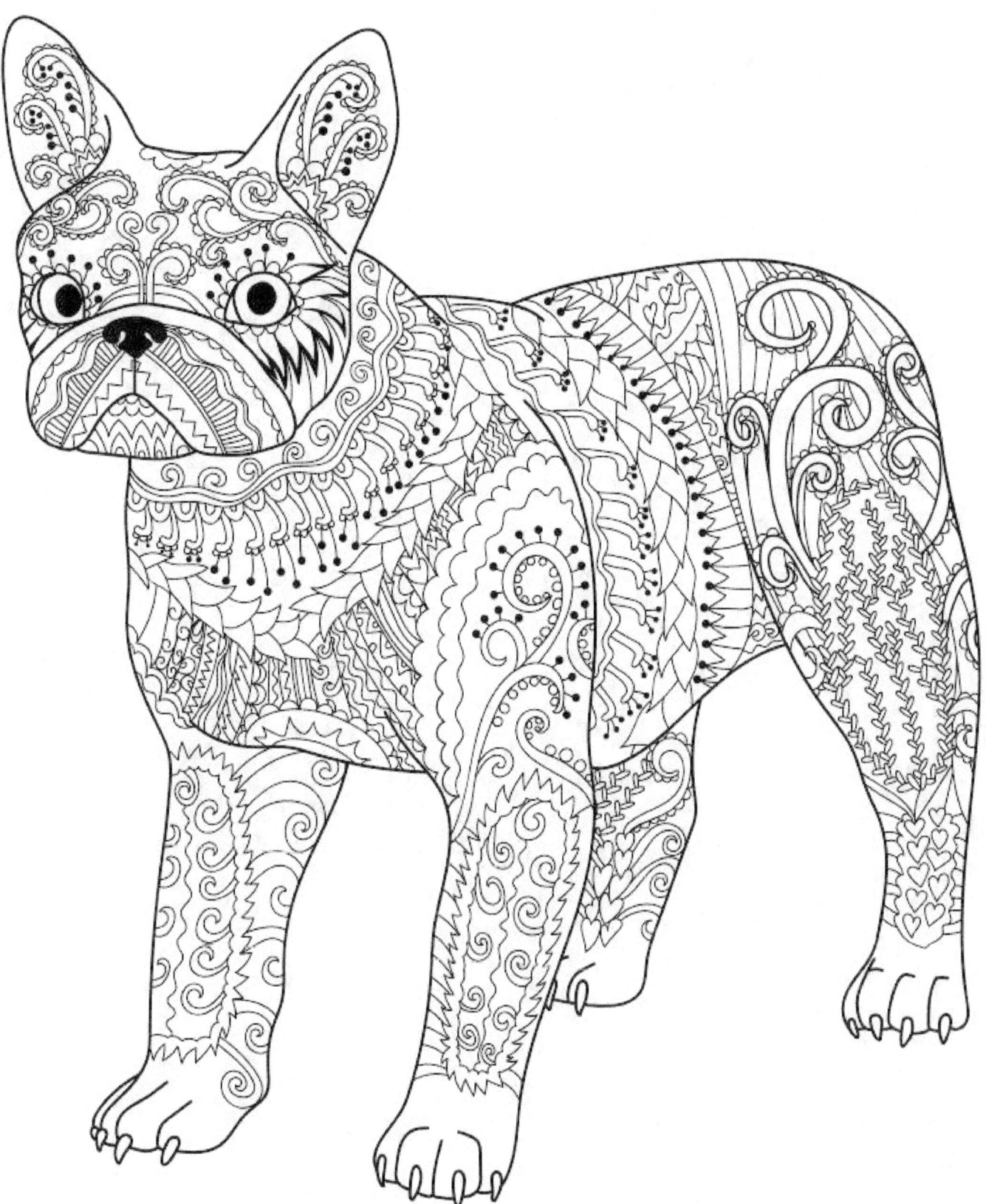

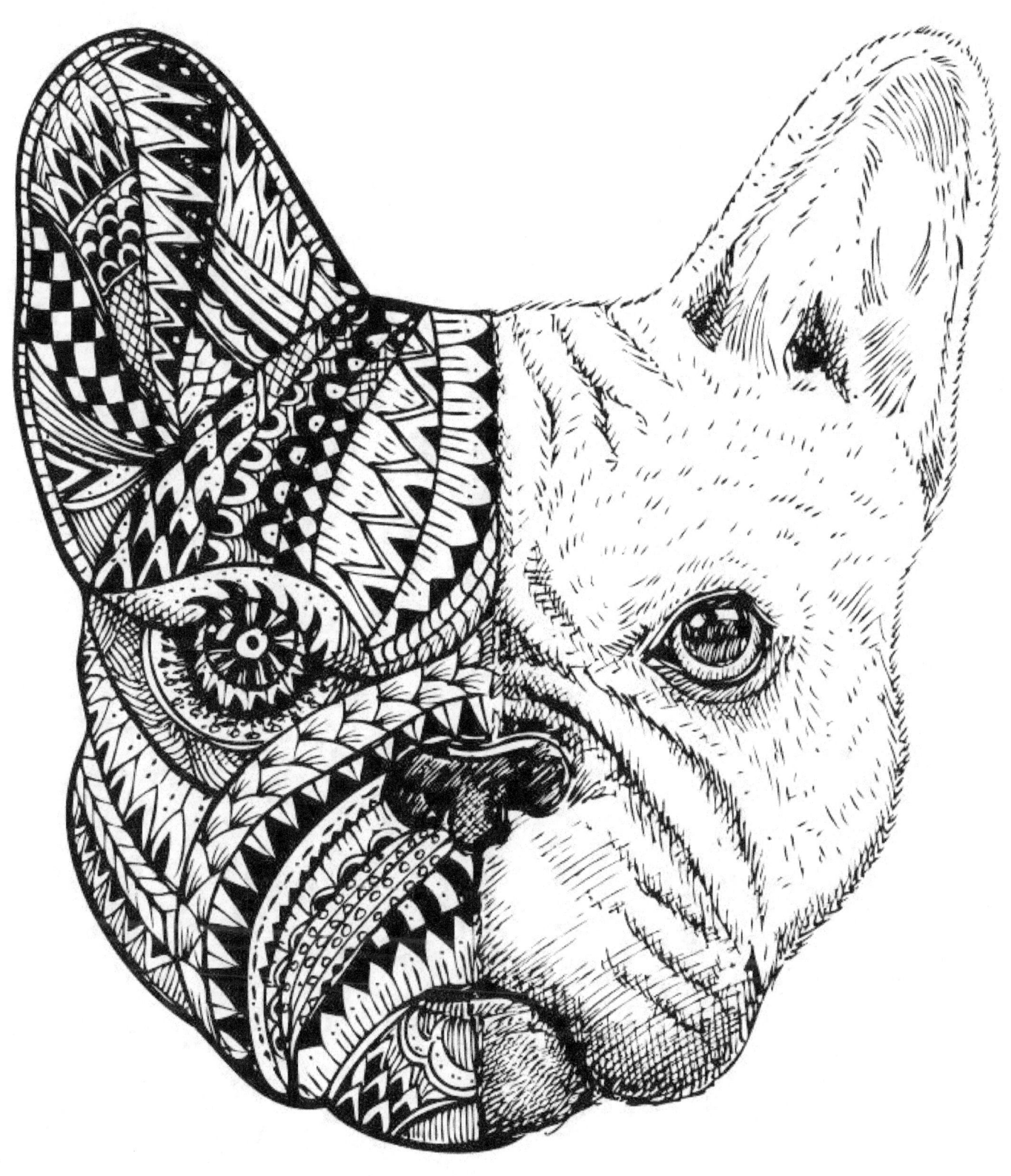

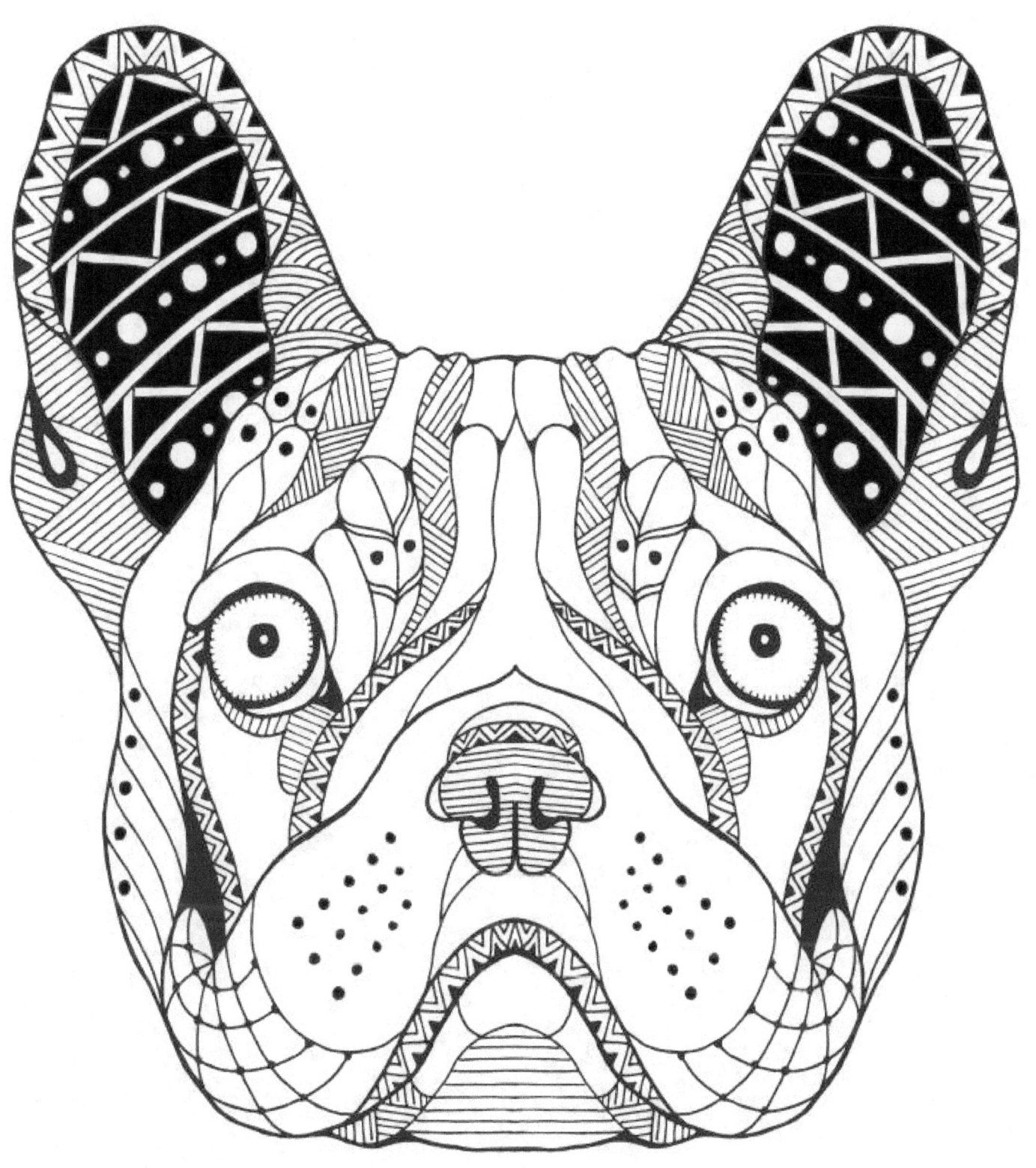

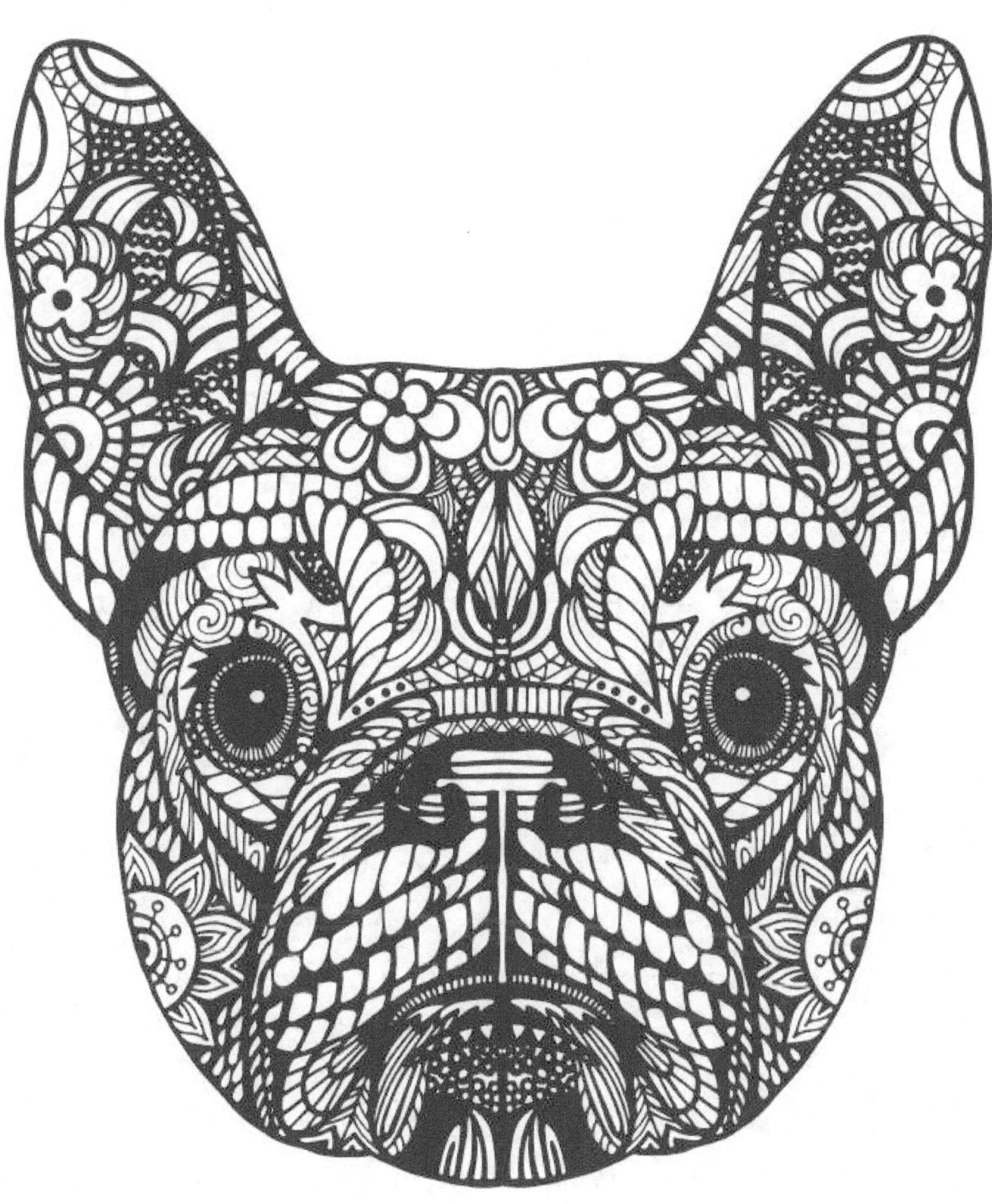

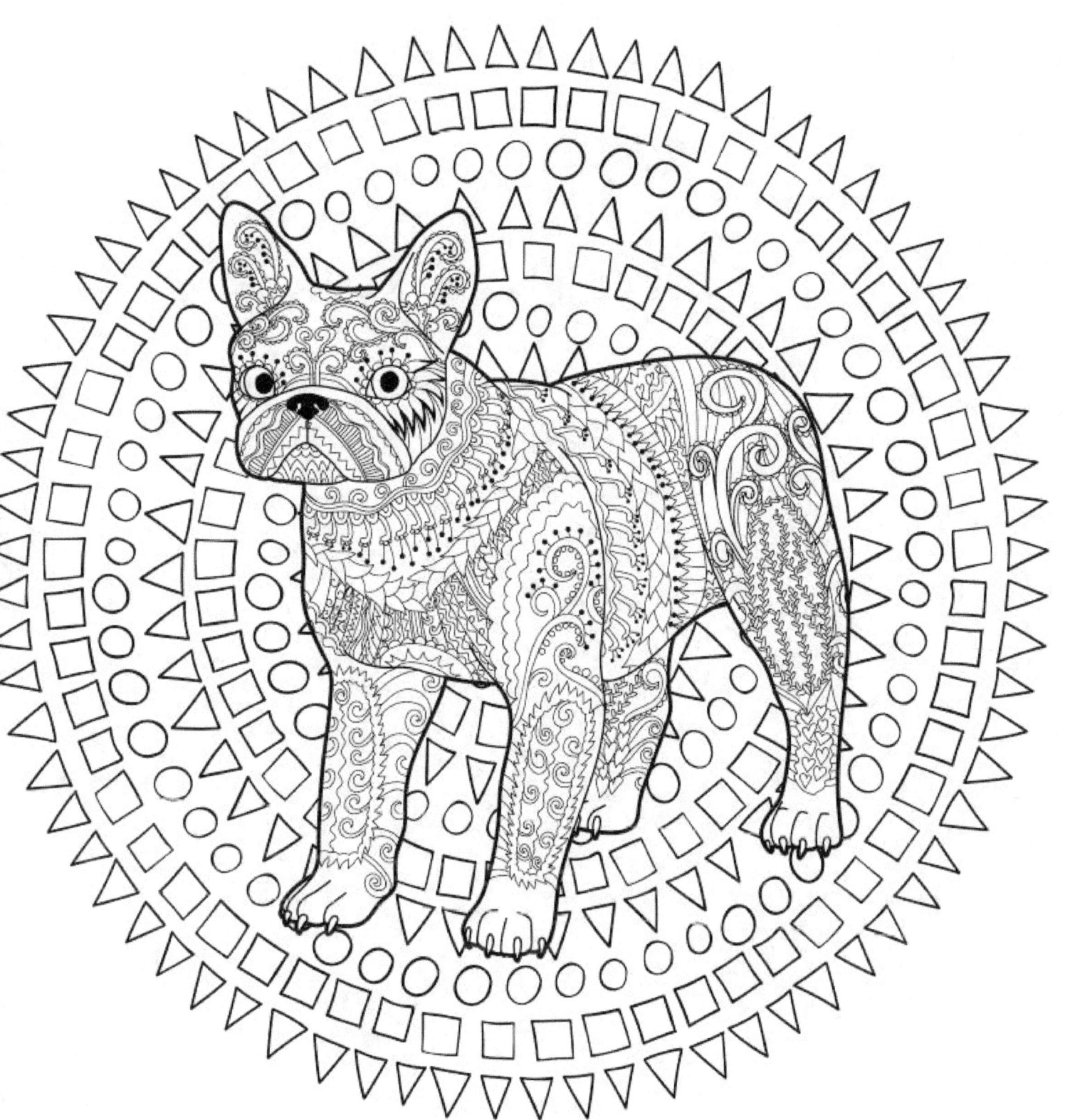

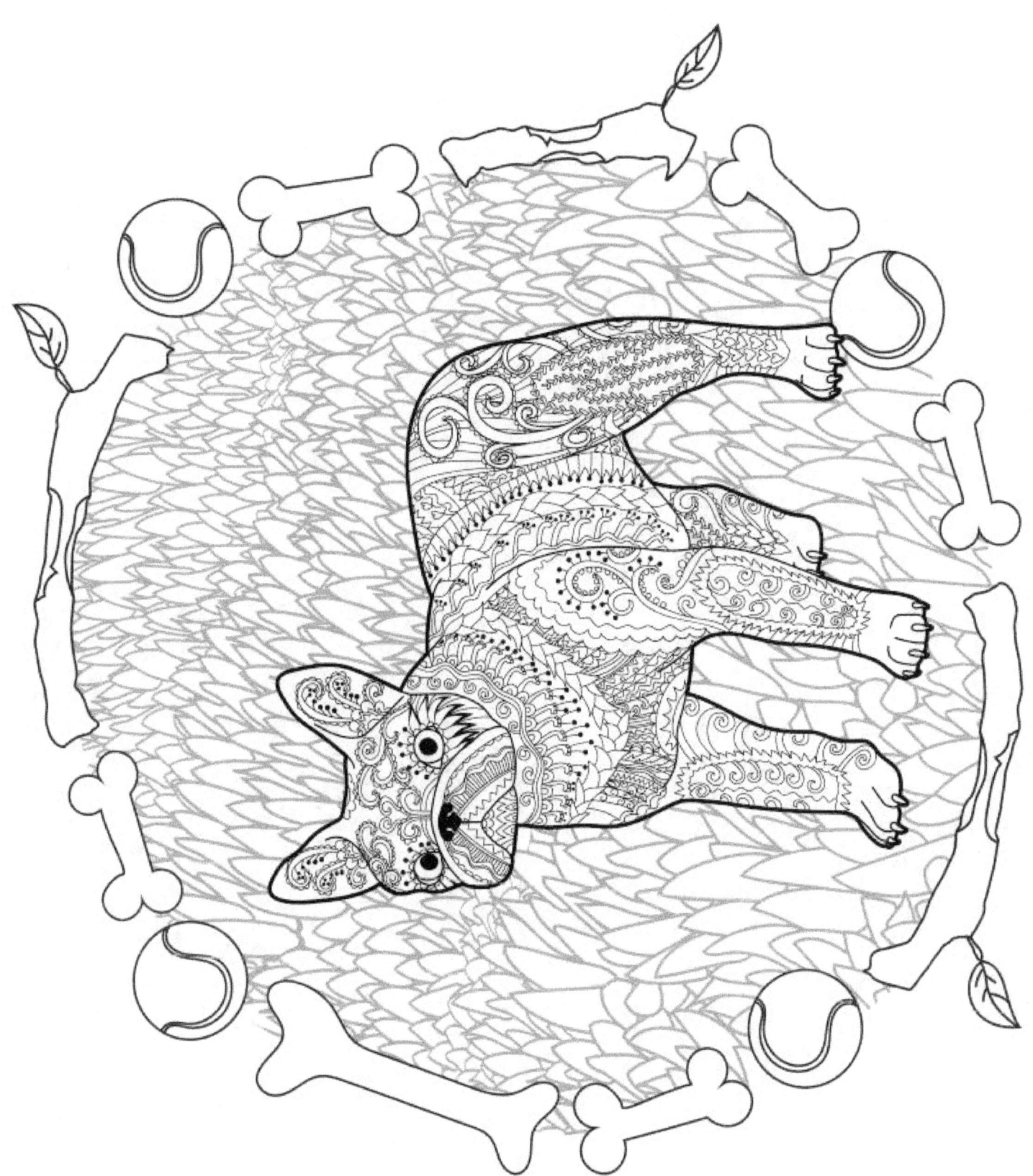

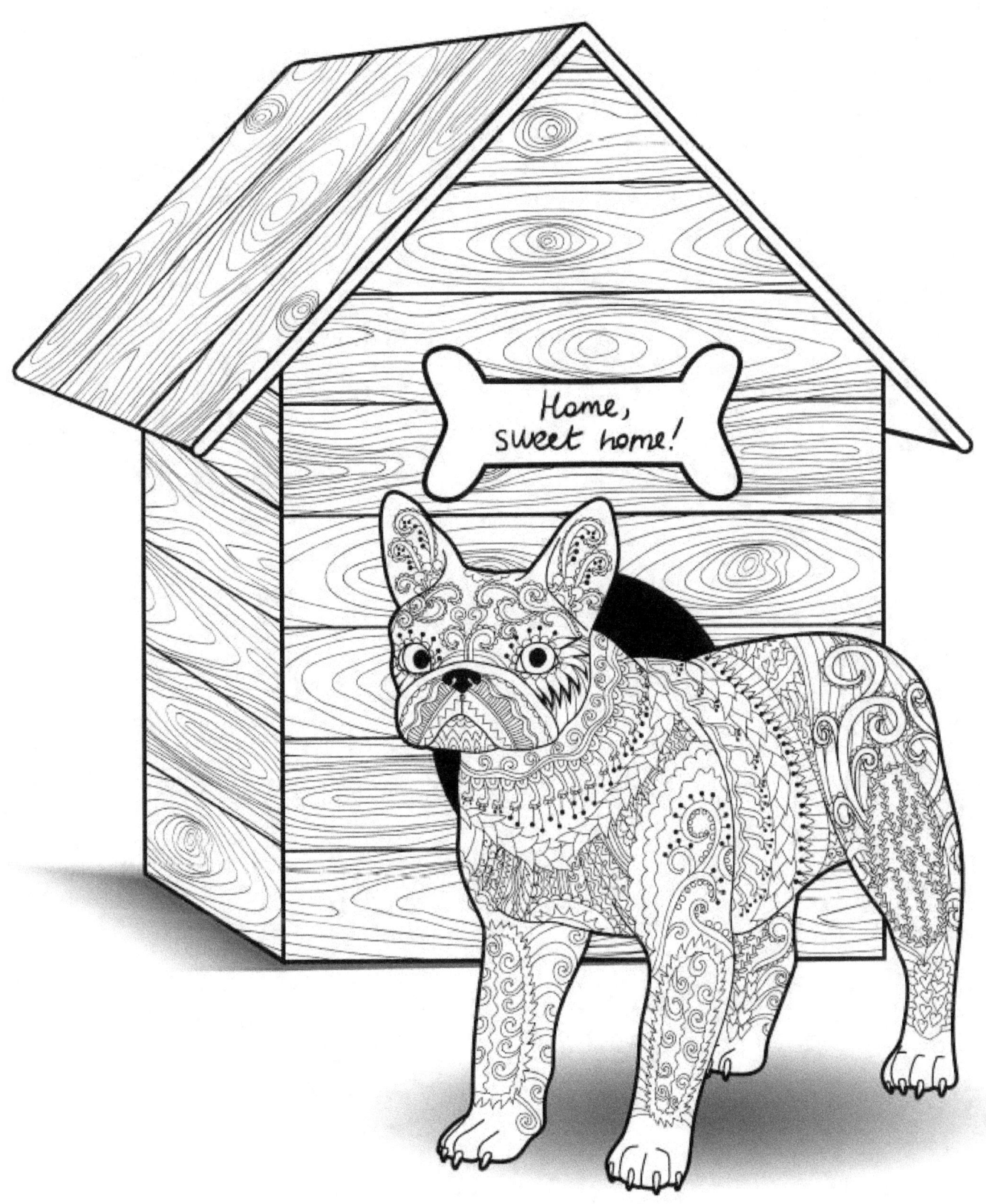

Surprise Bonus Dog Breeds and Beautiful Sea Turtles Coloring Pages!

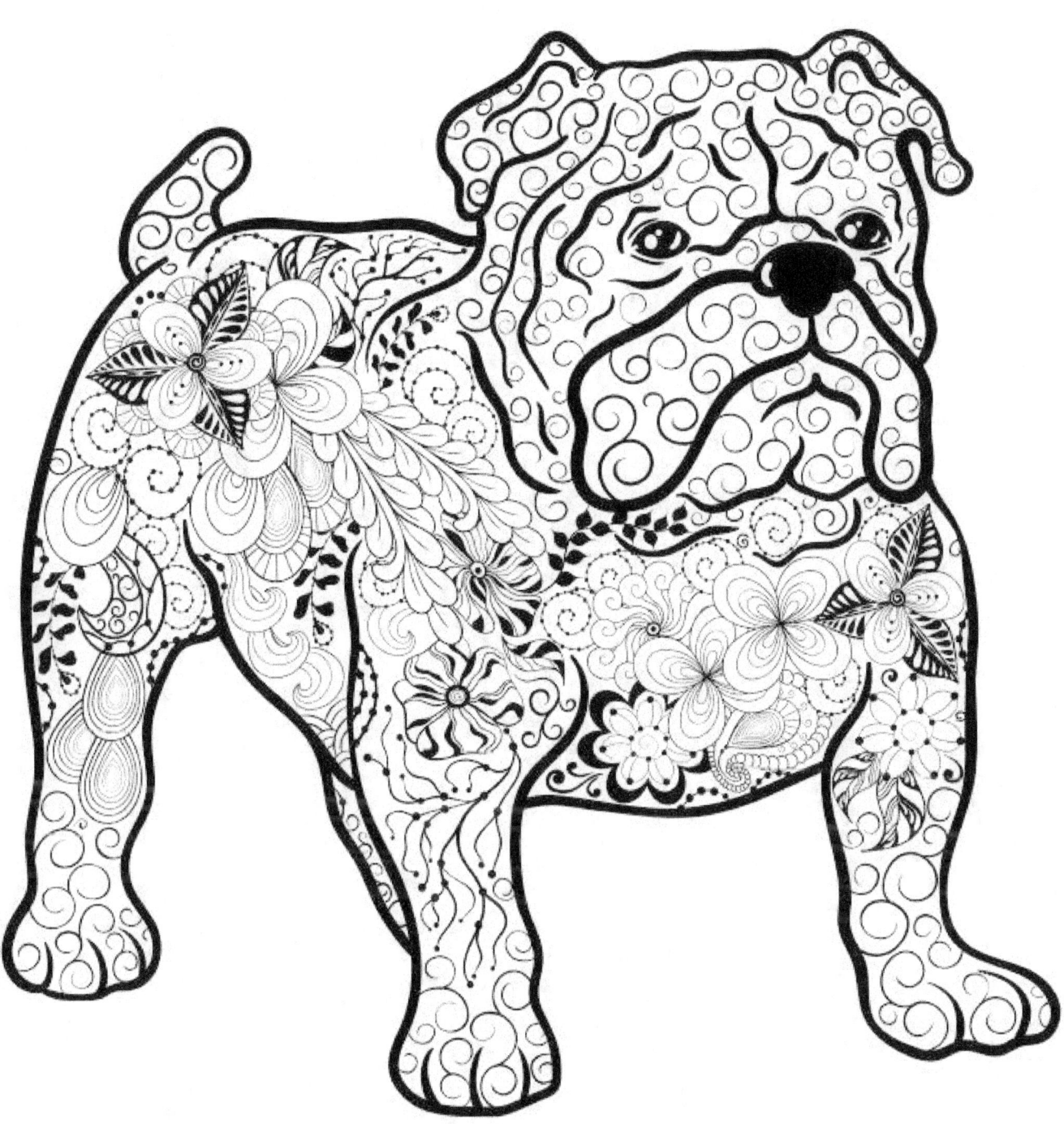

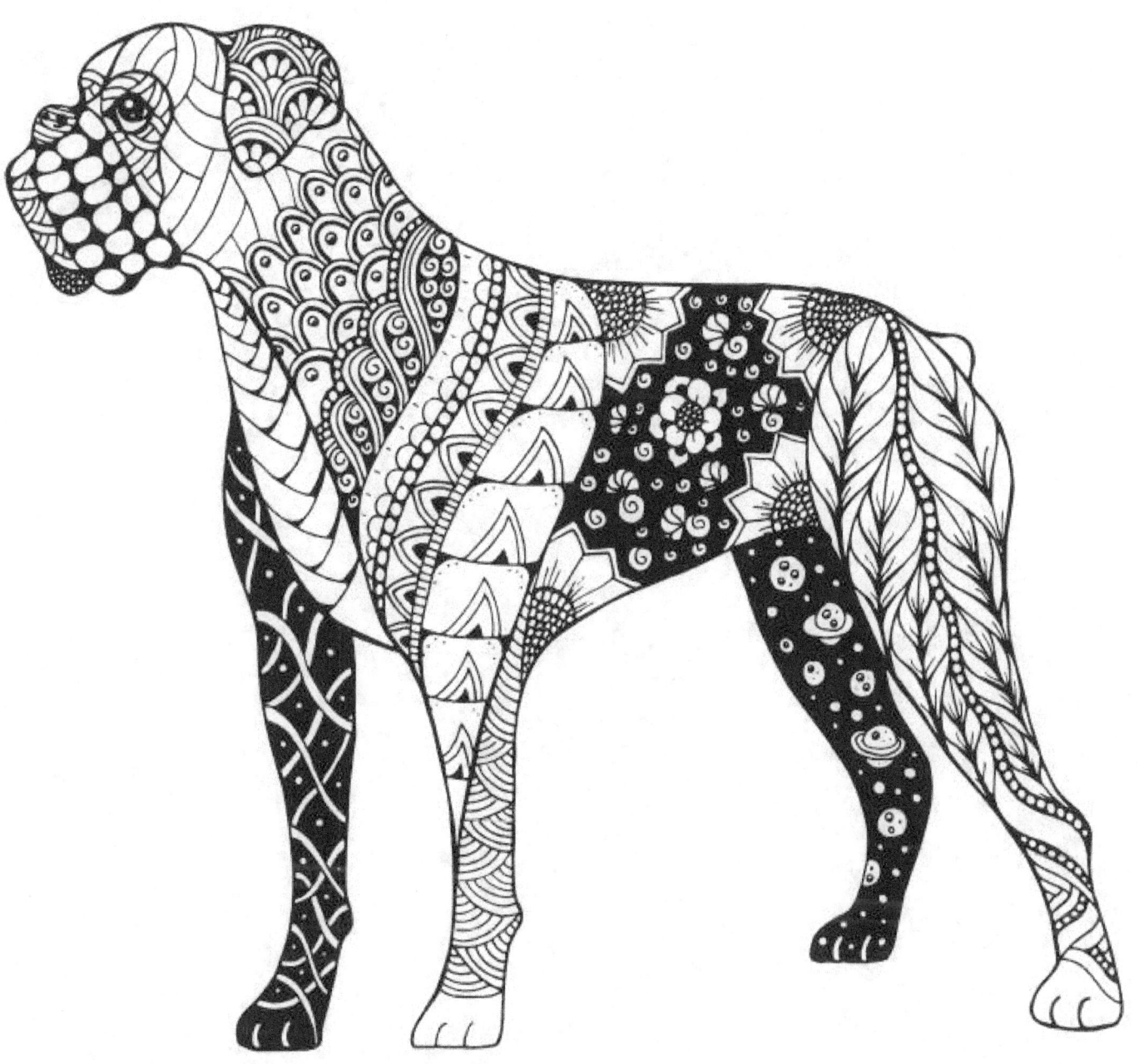

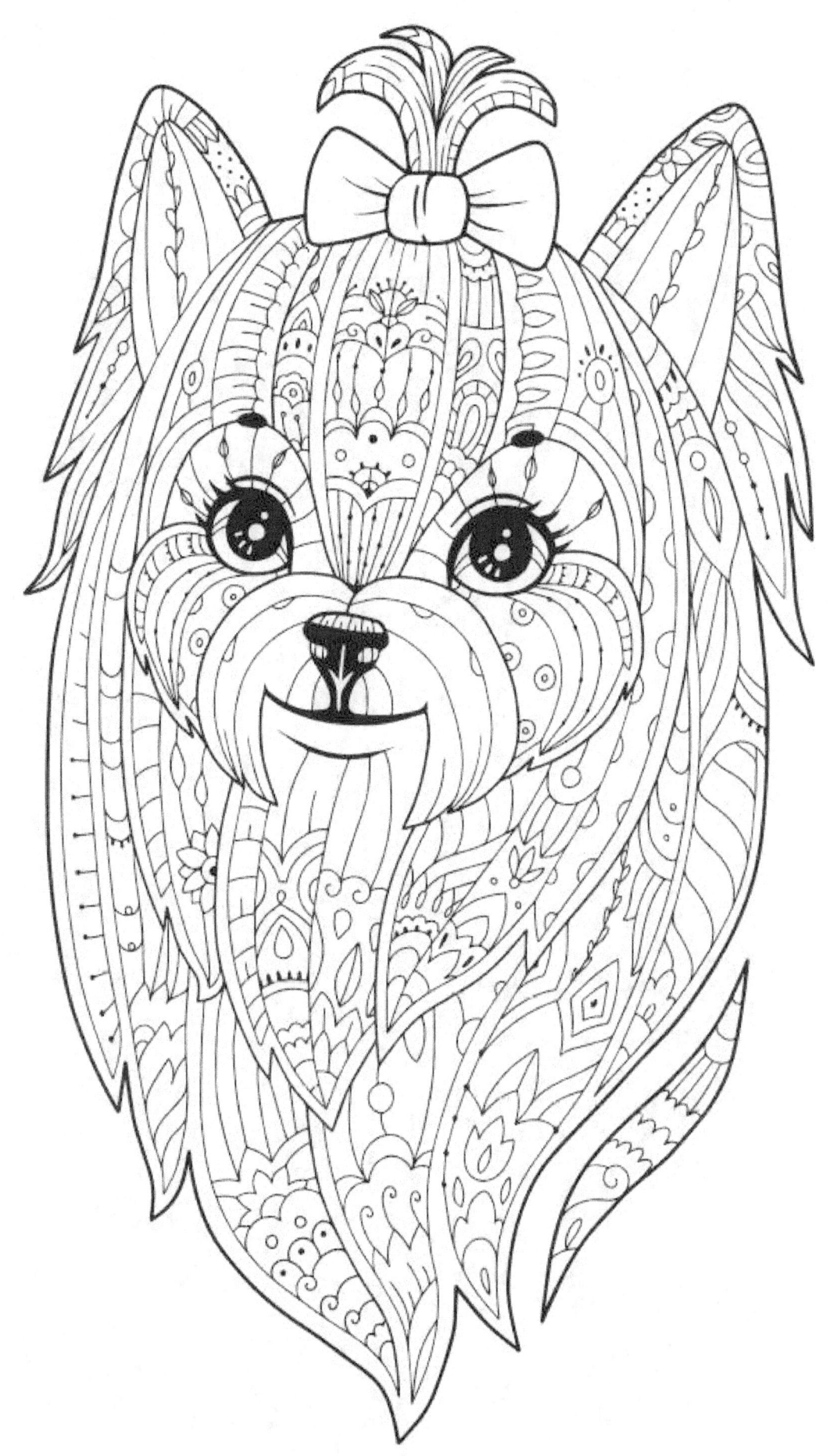

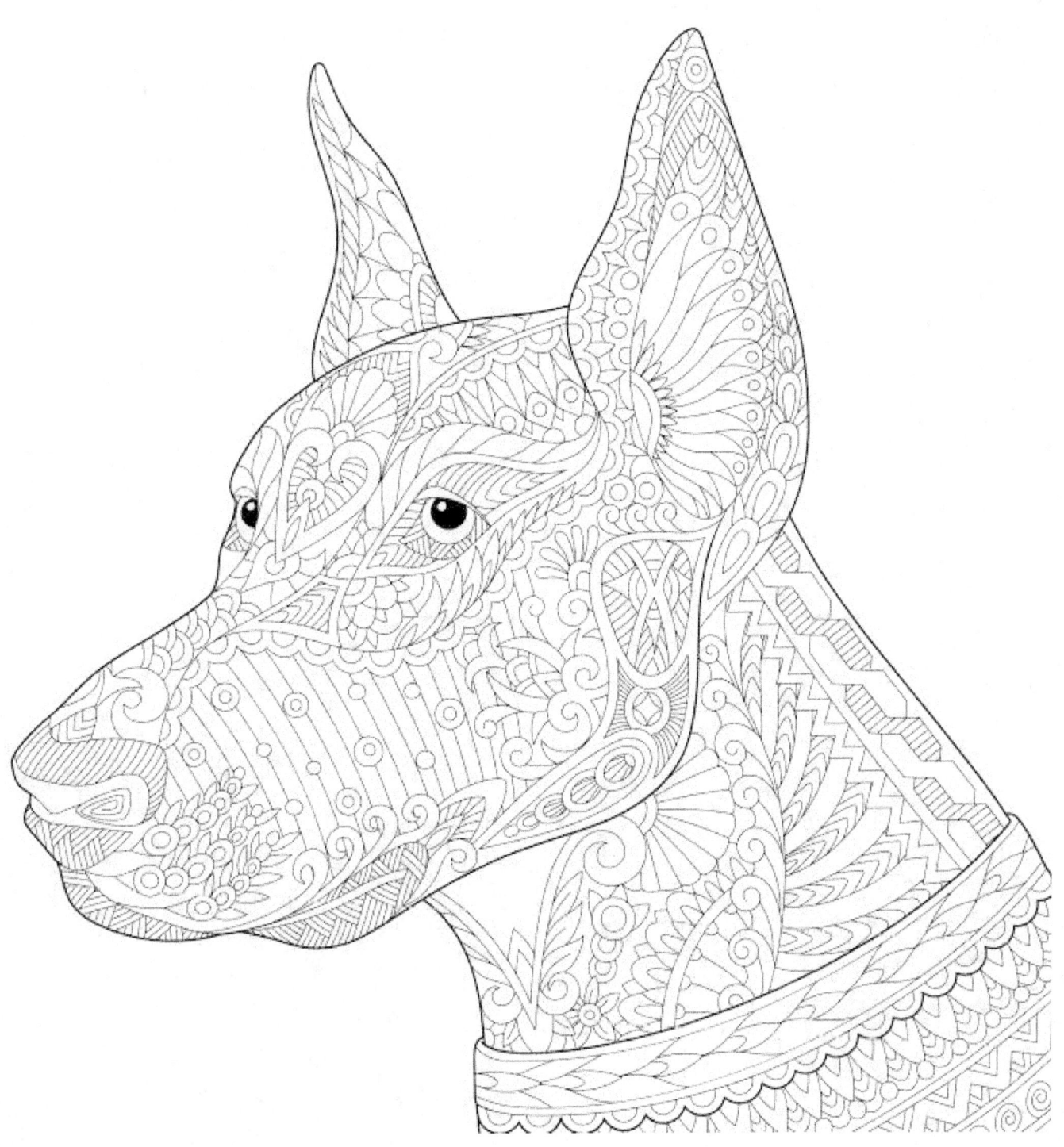

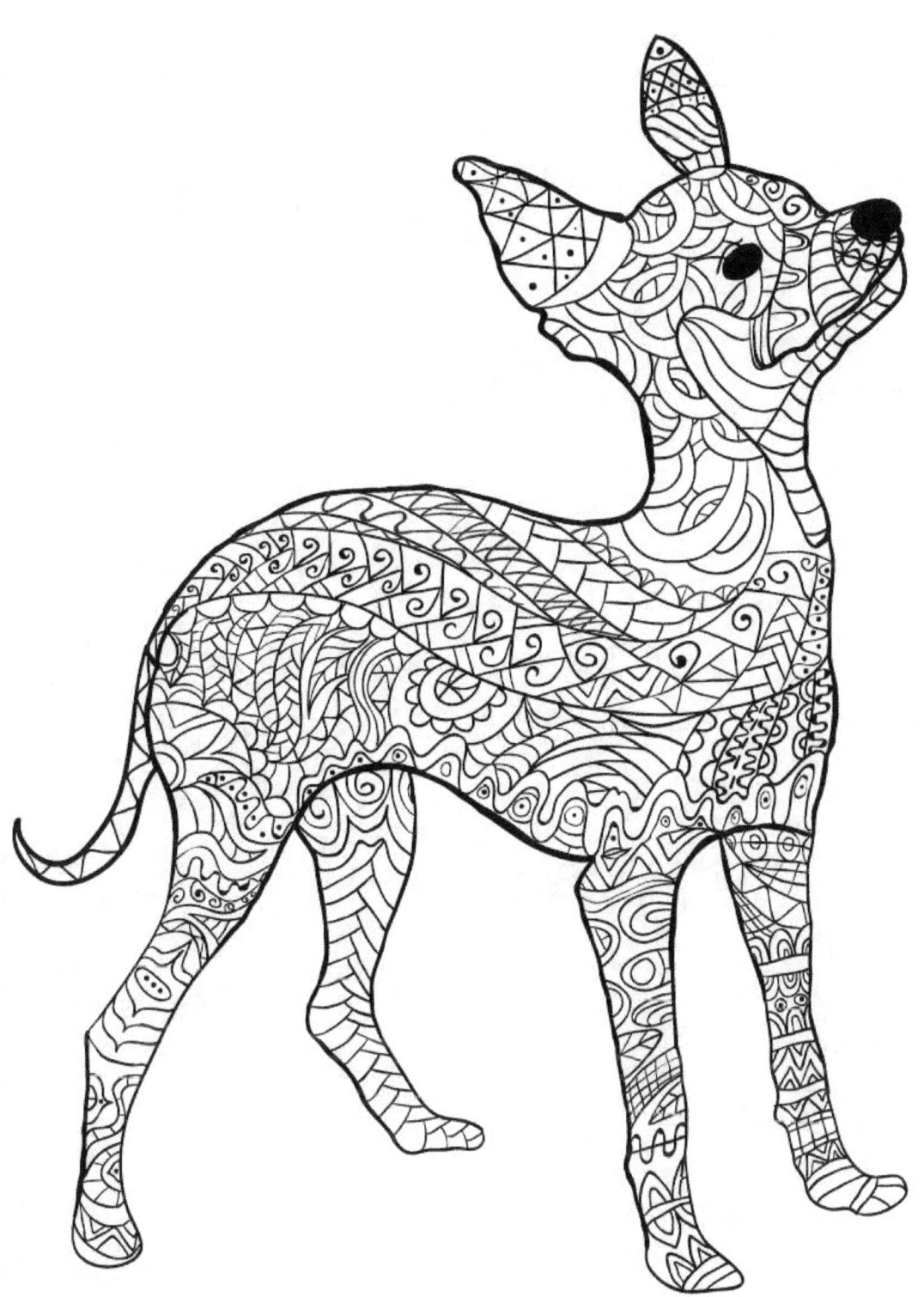

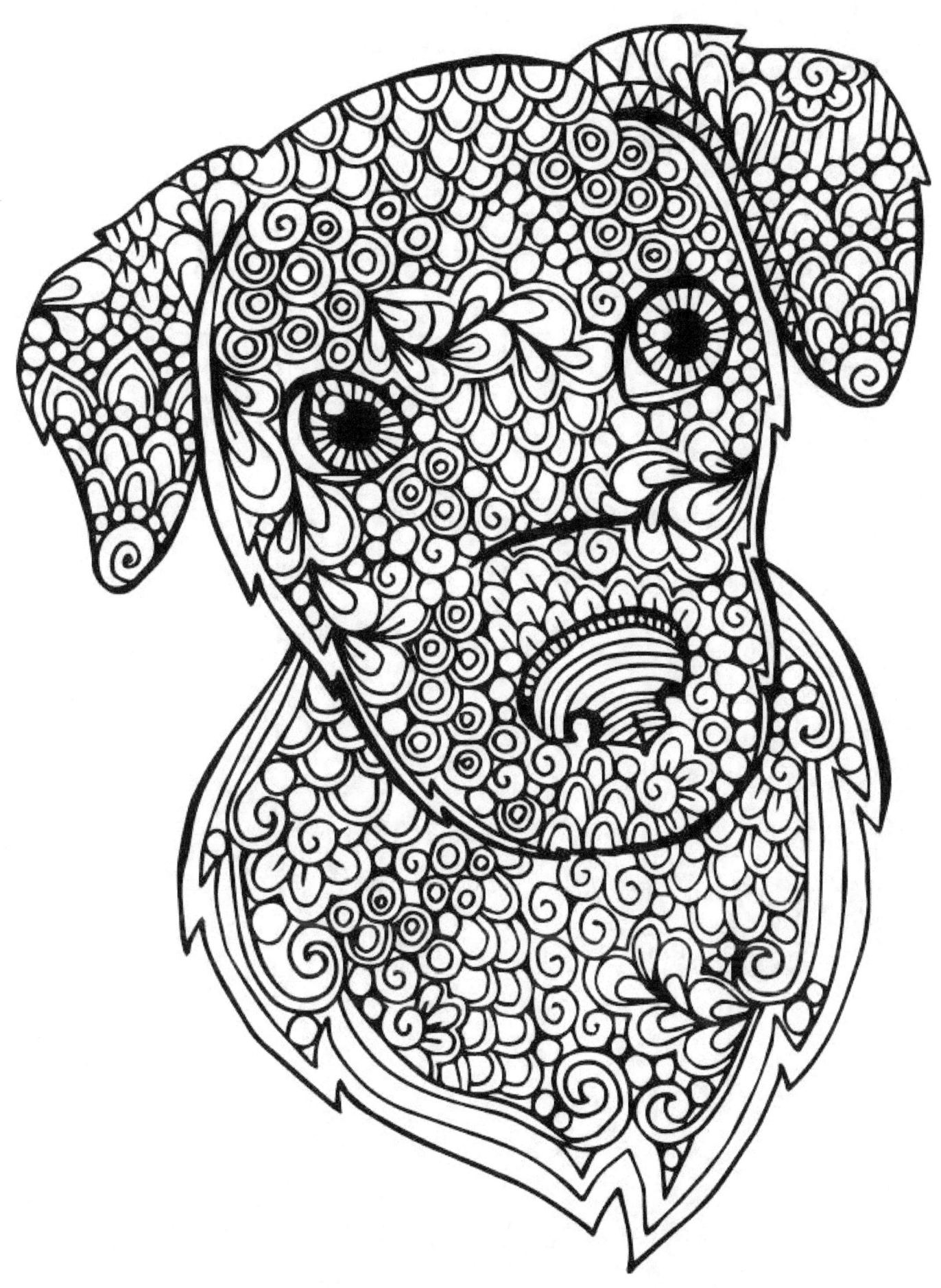

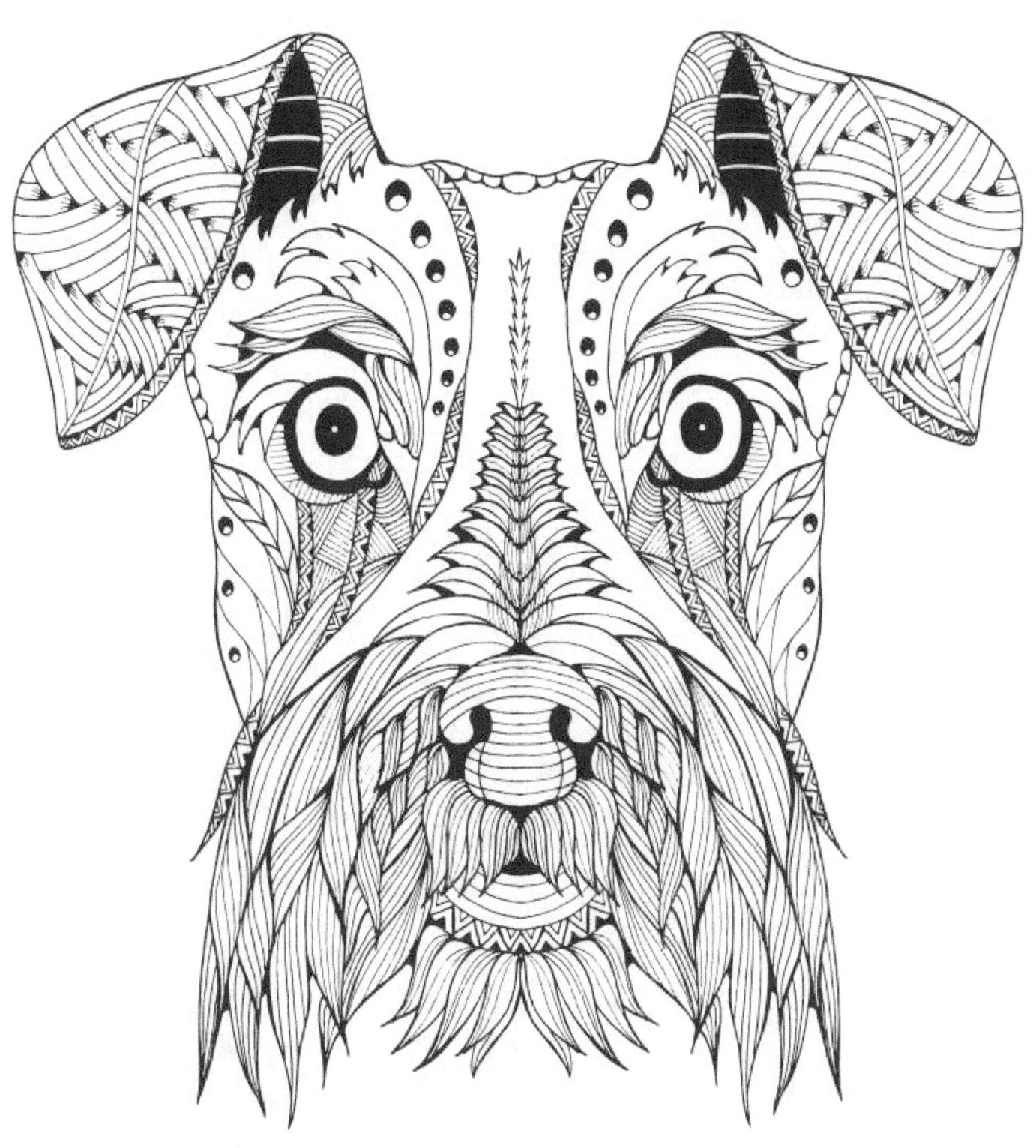

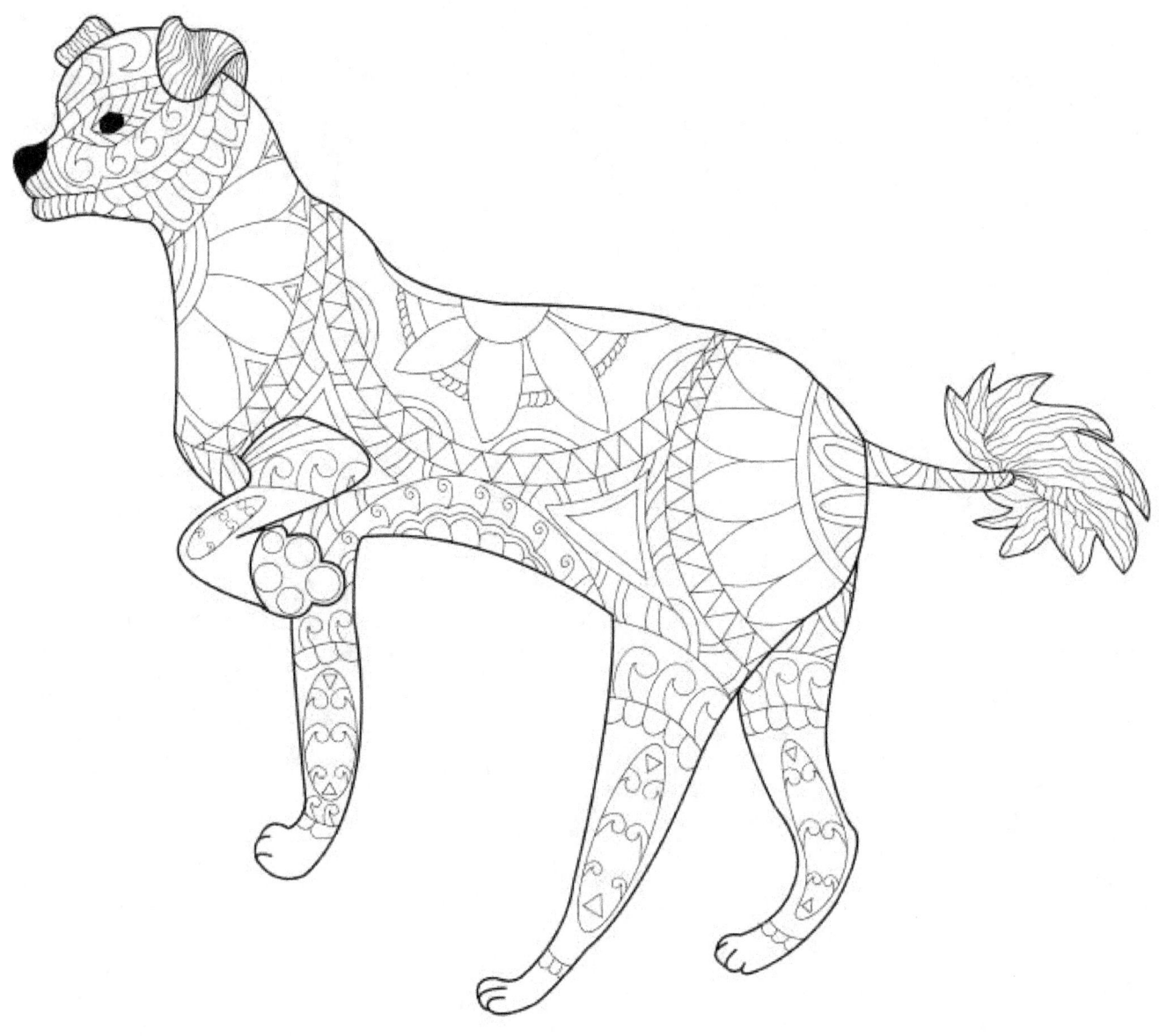

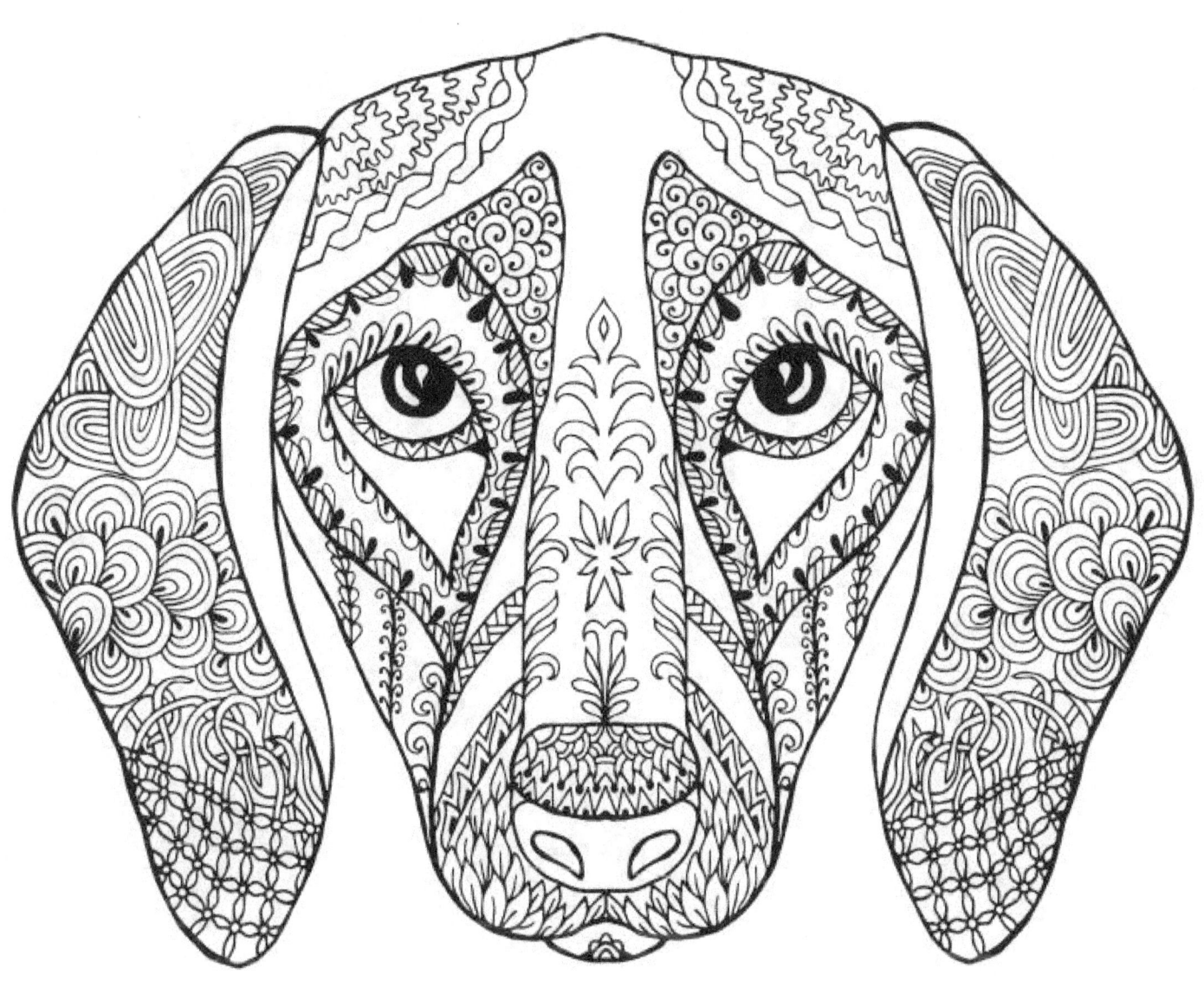

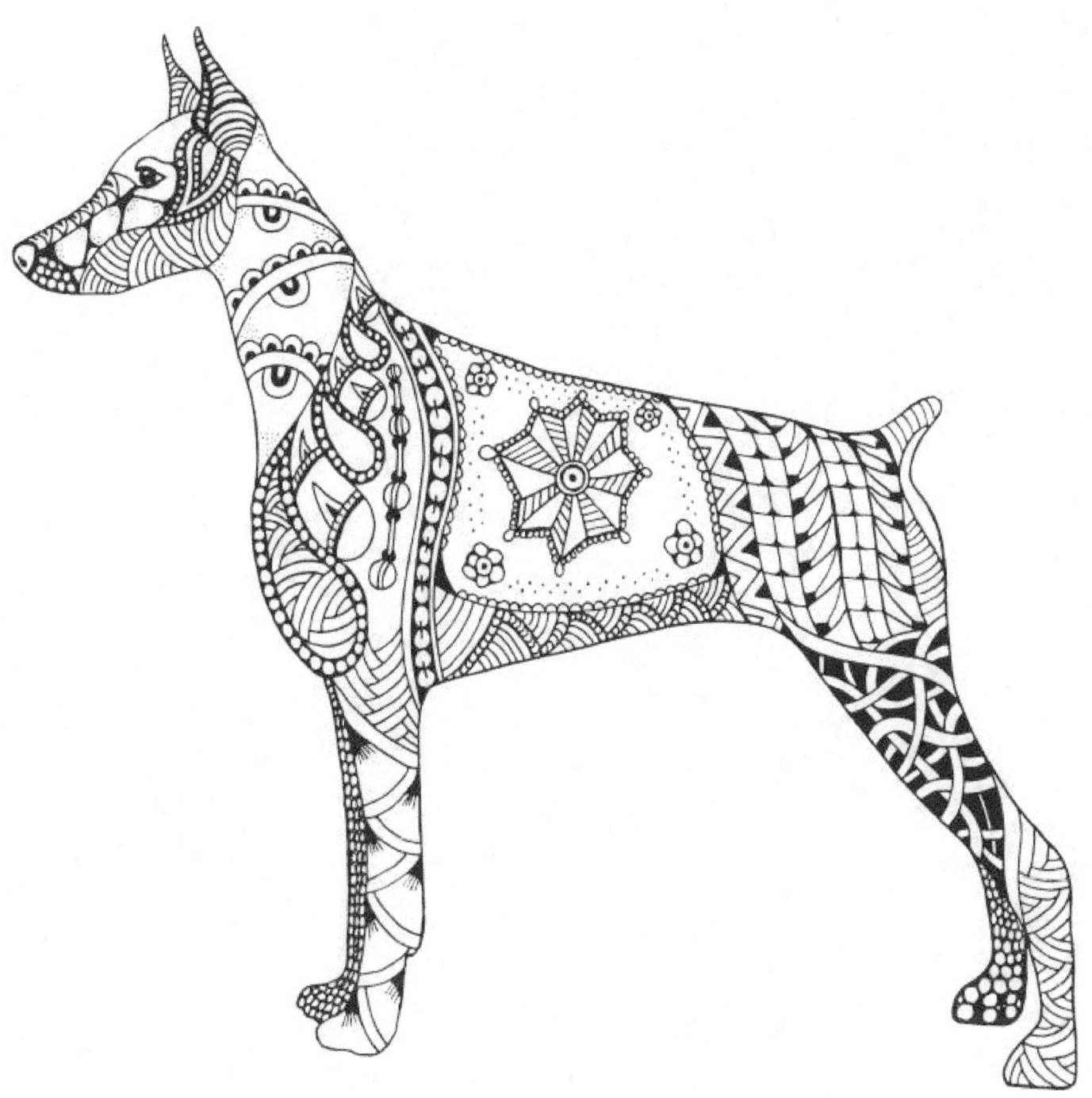

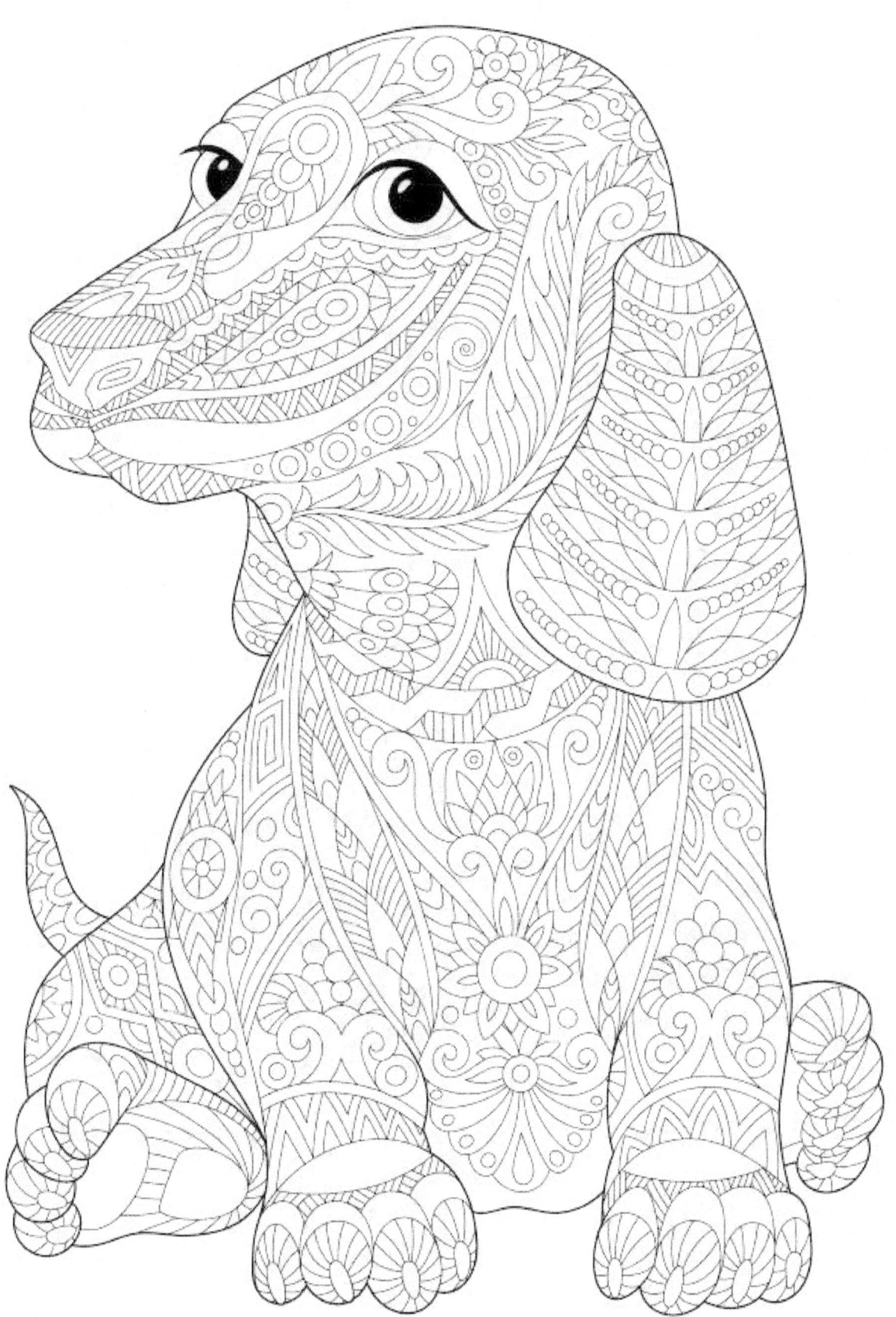

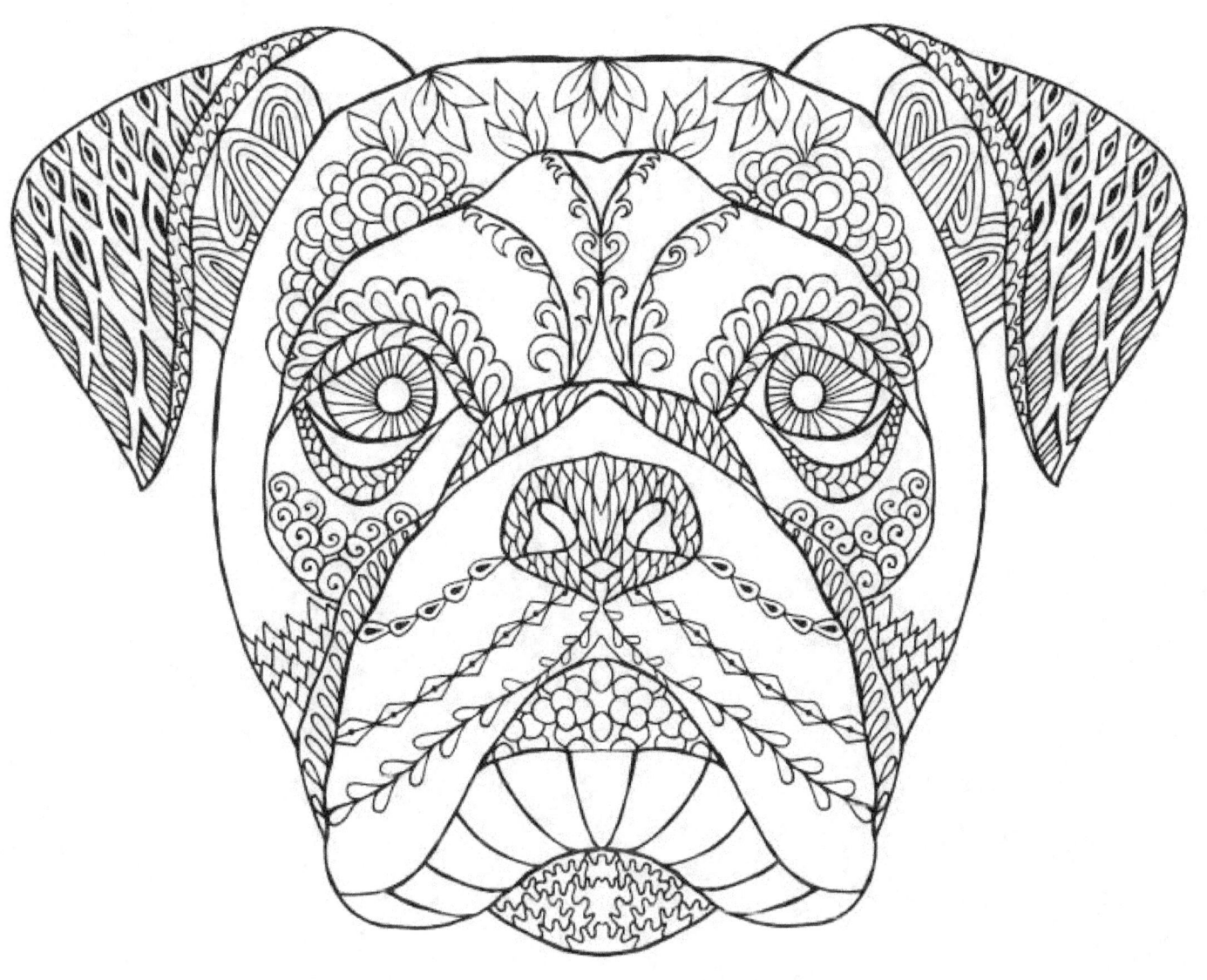

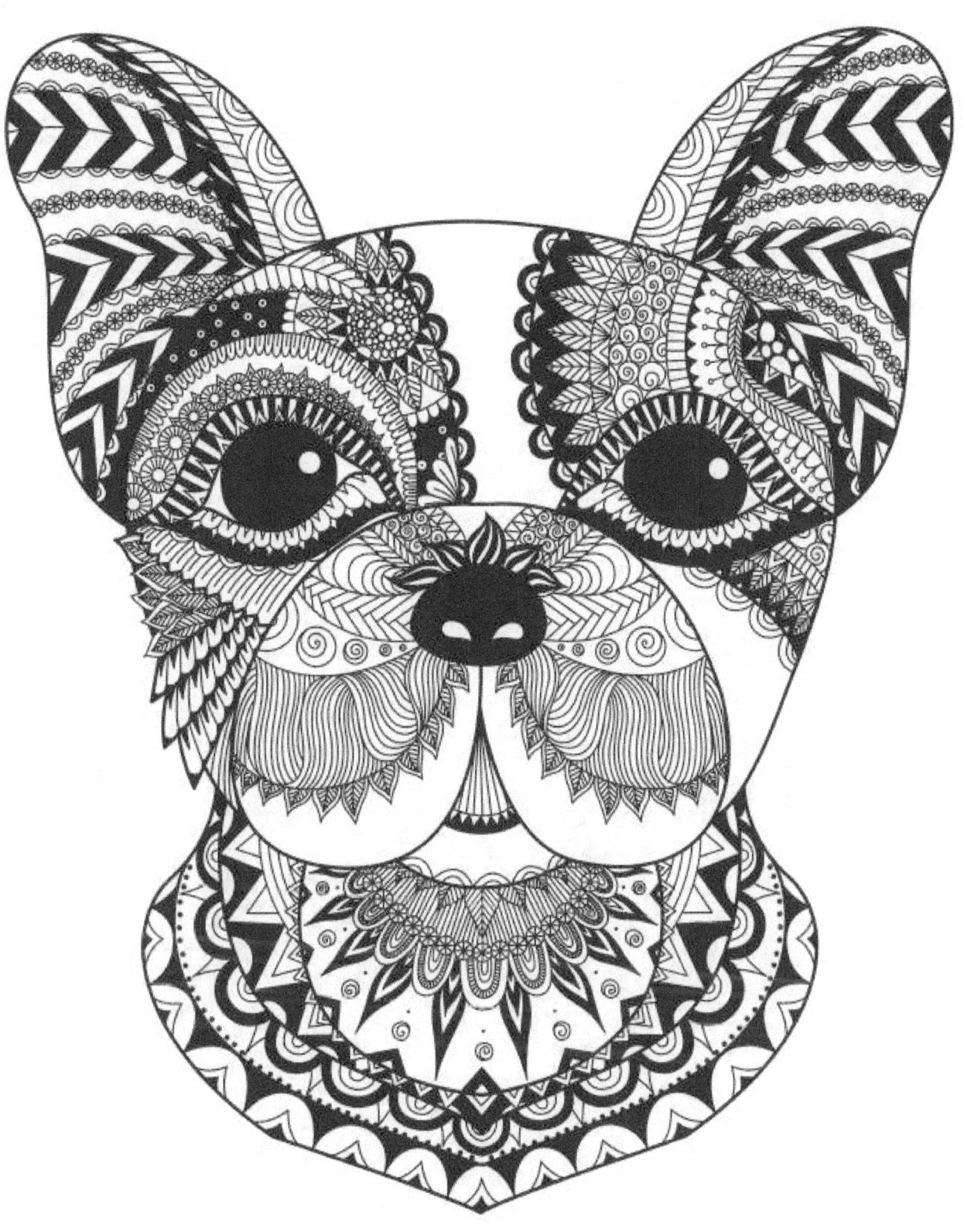

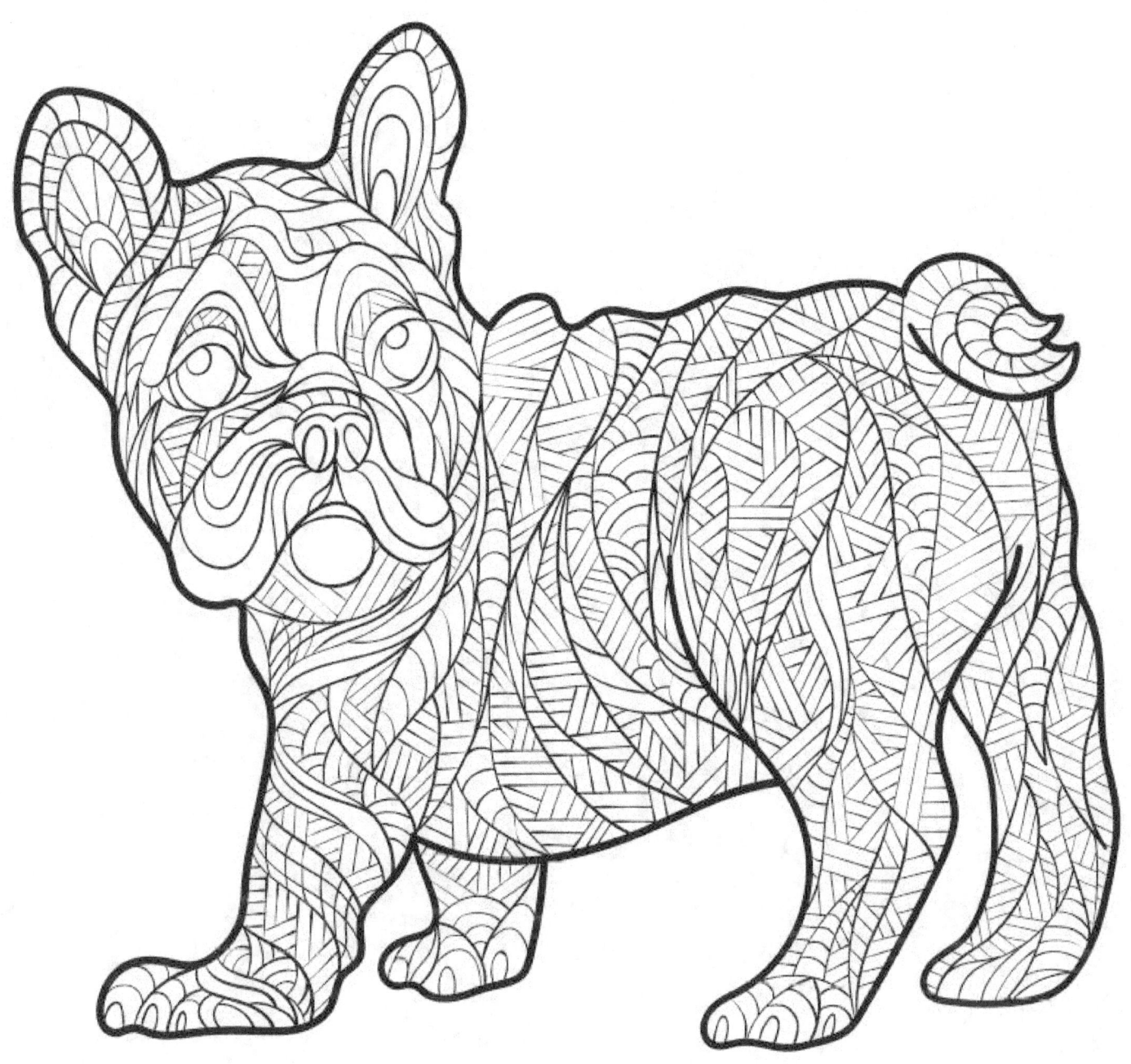

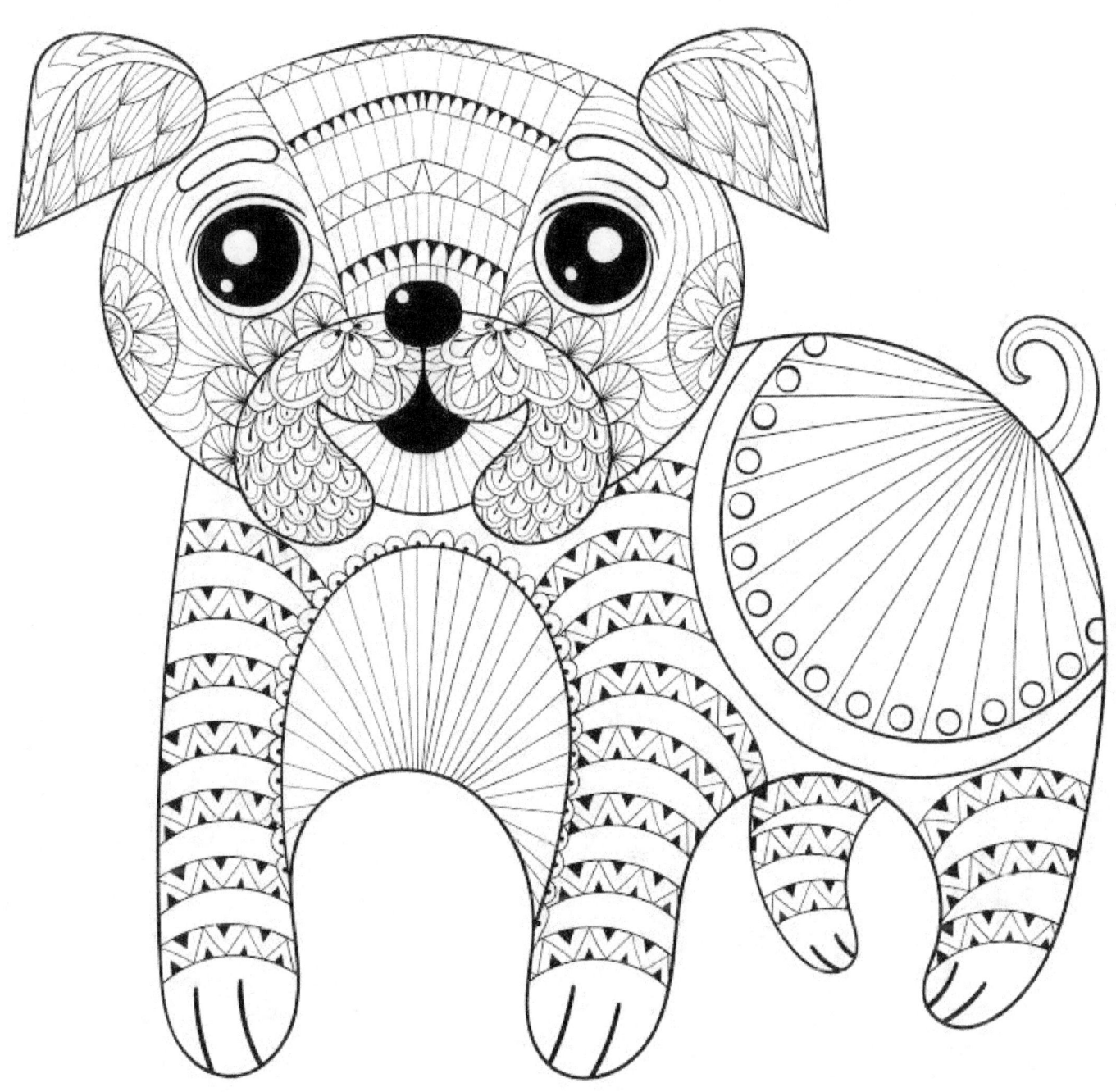

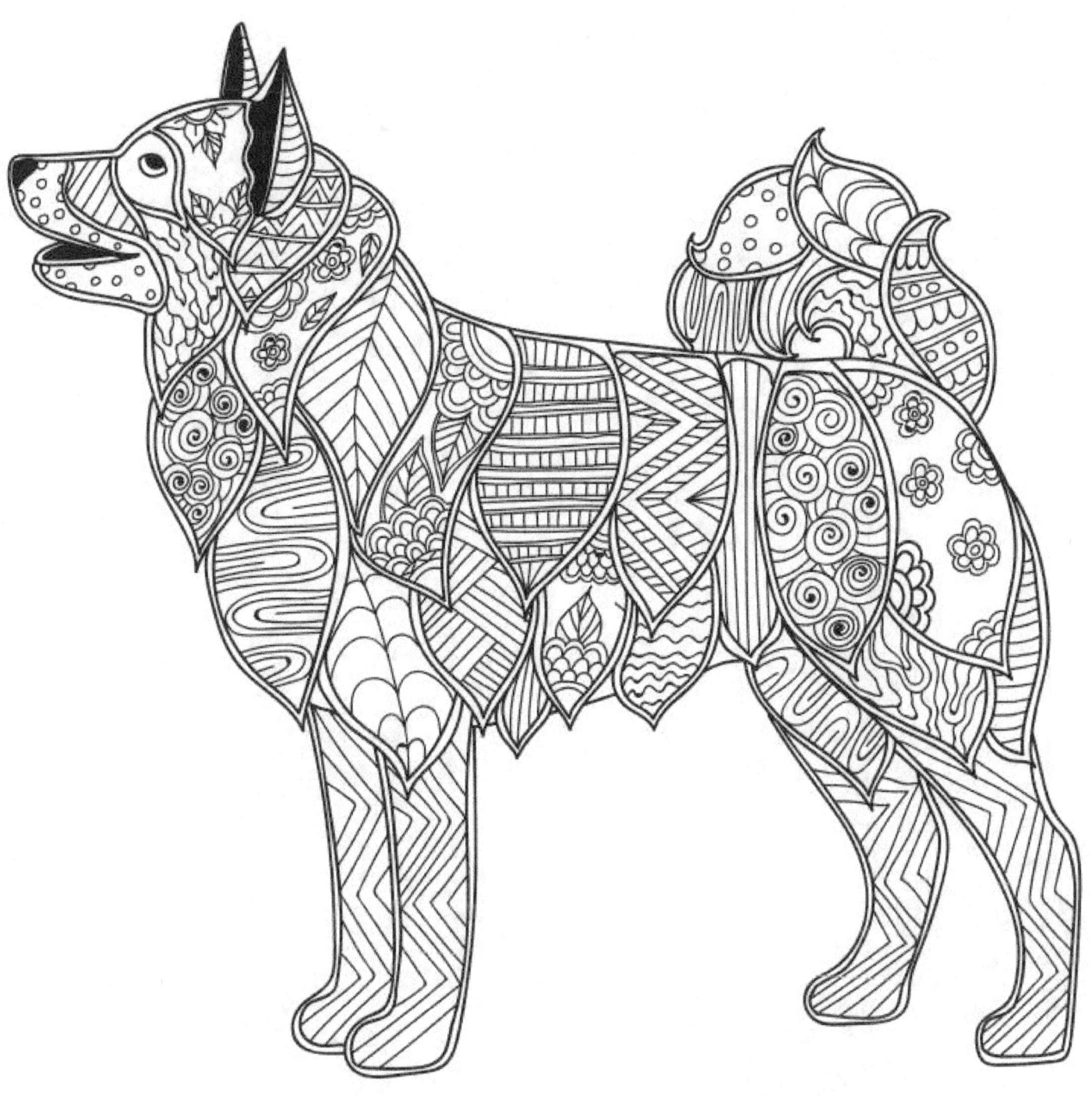

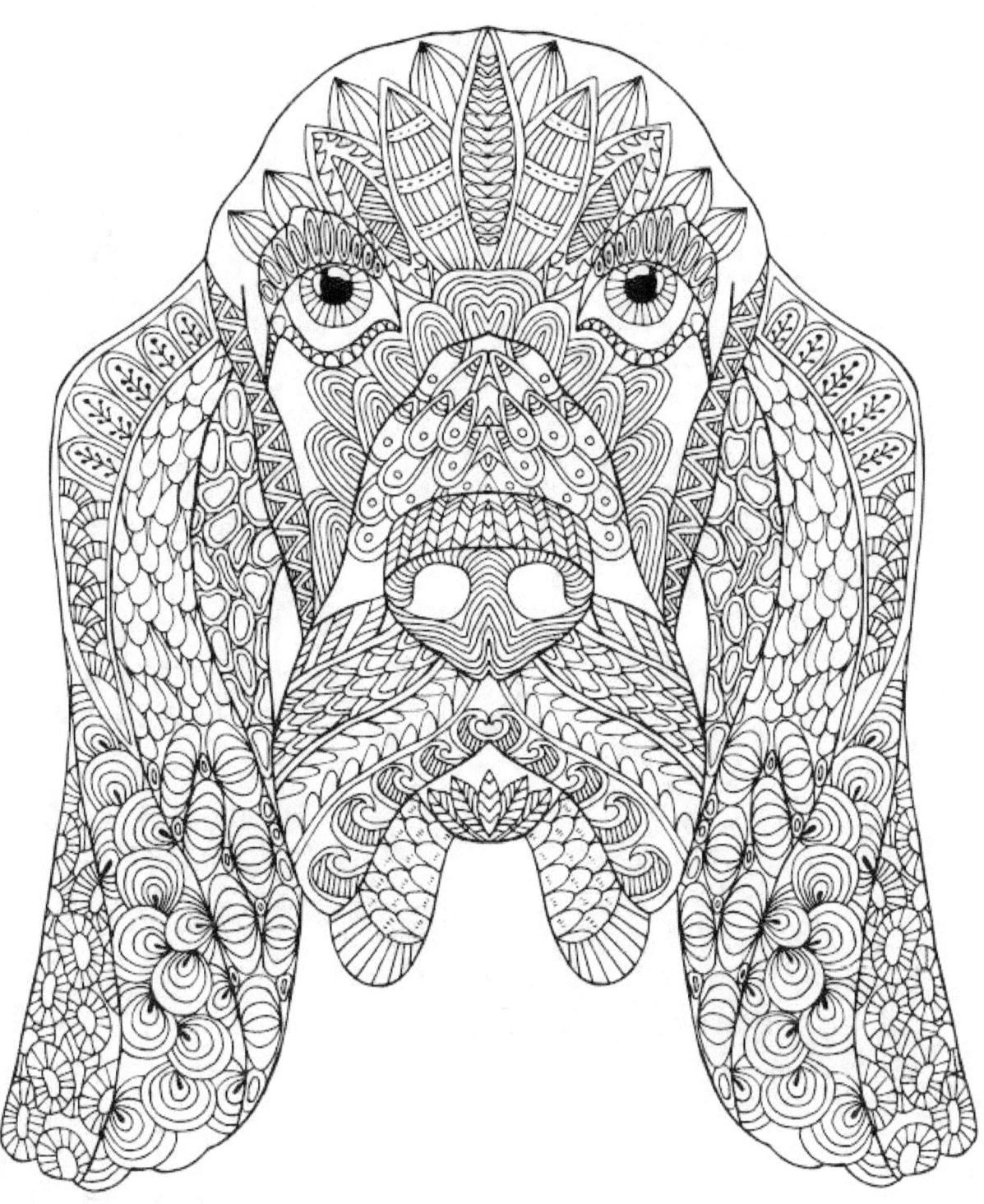

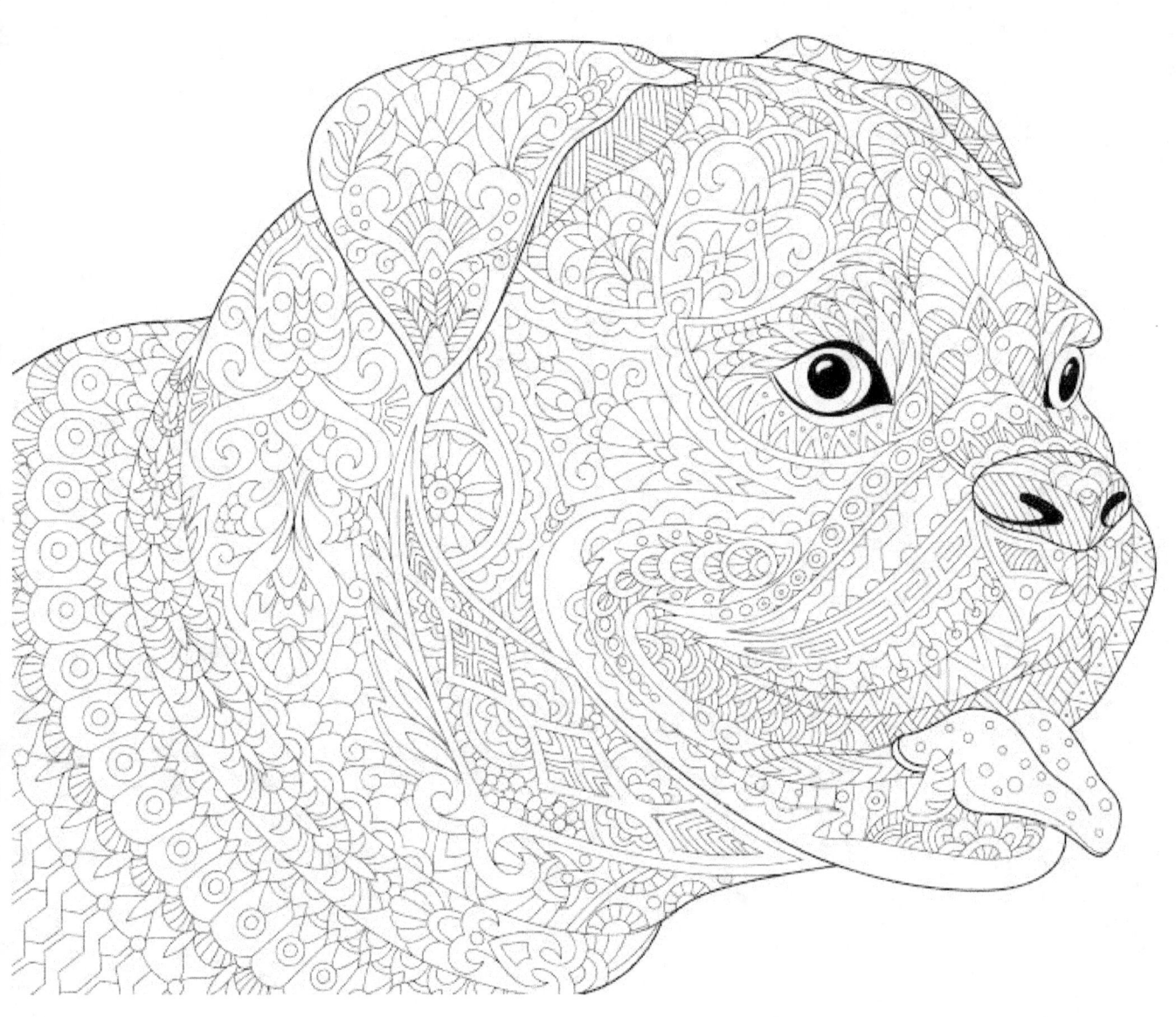

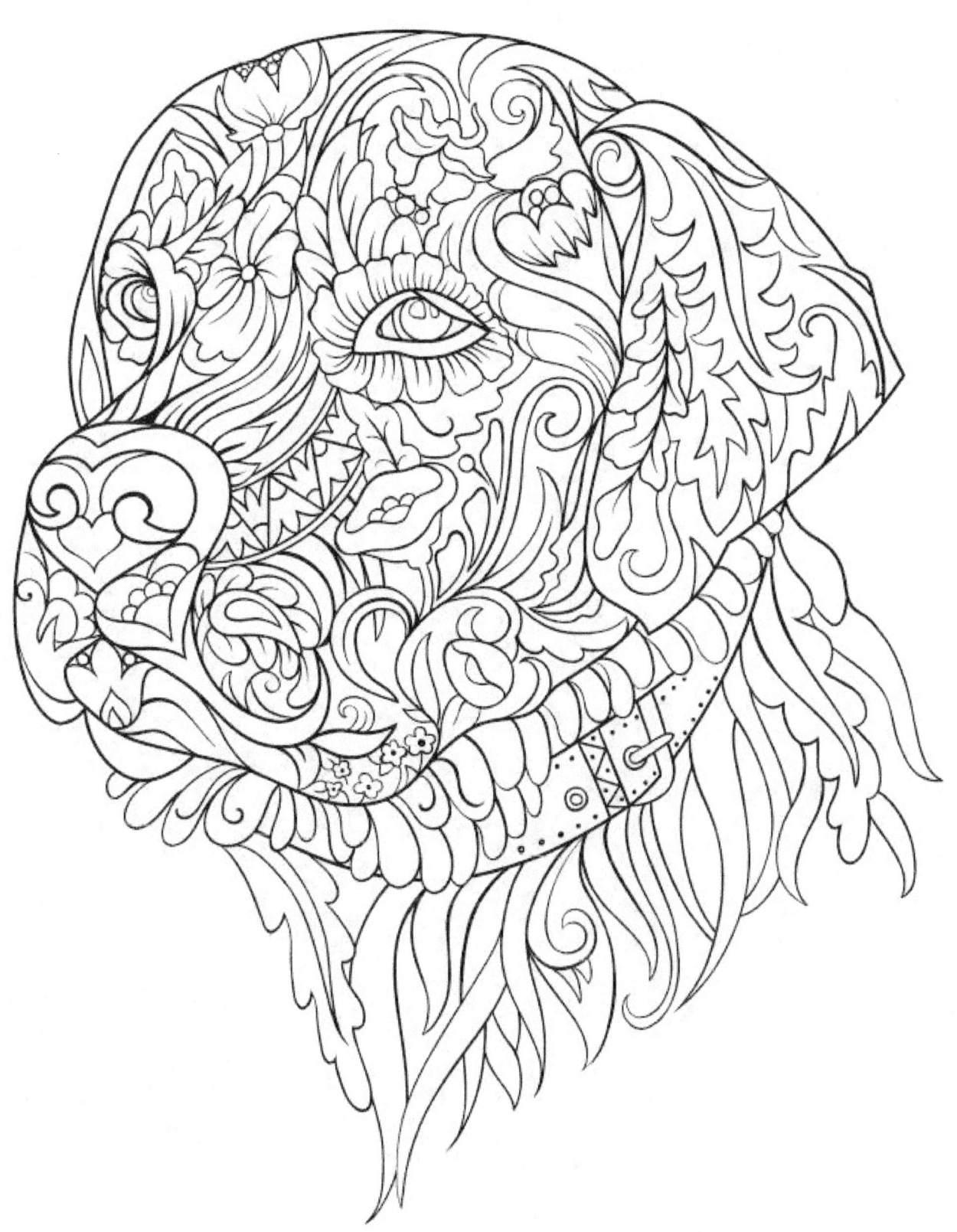

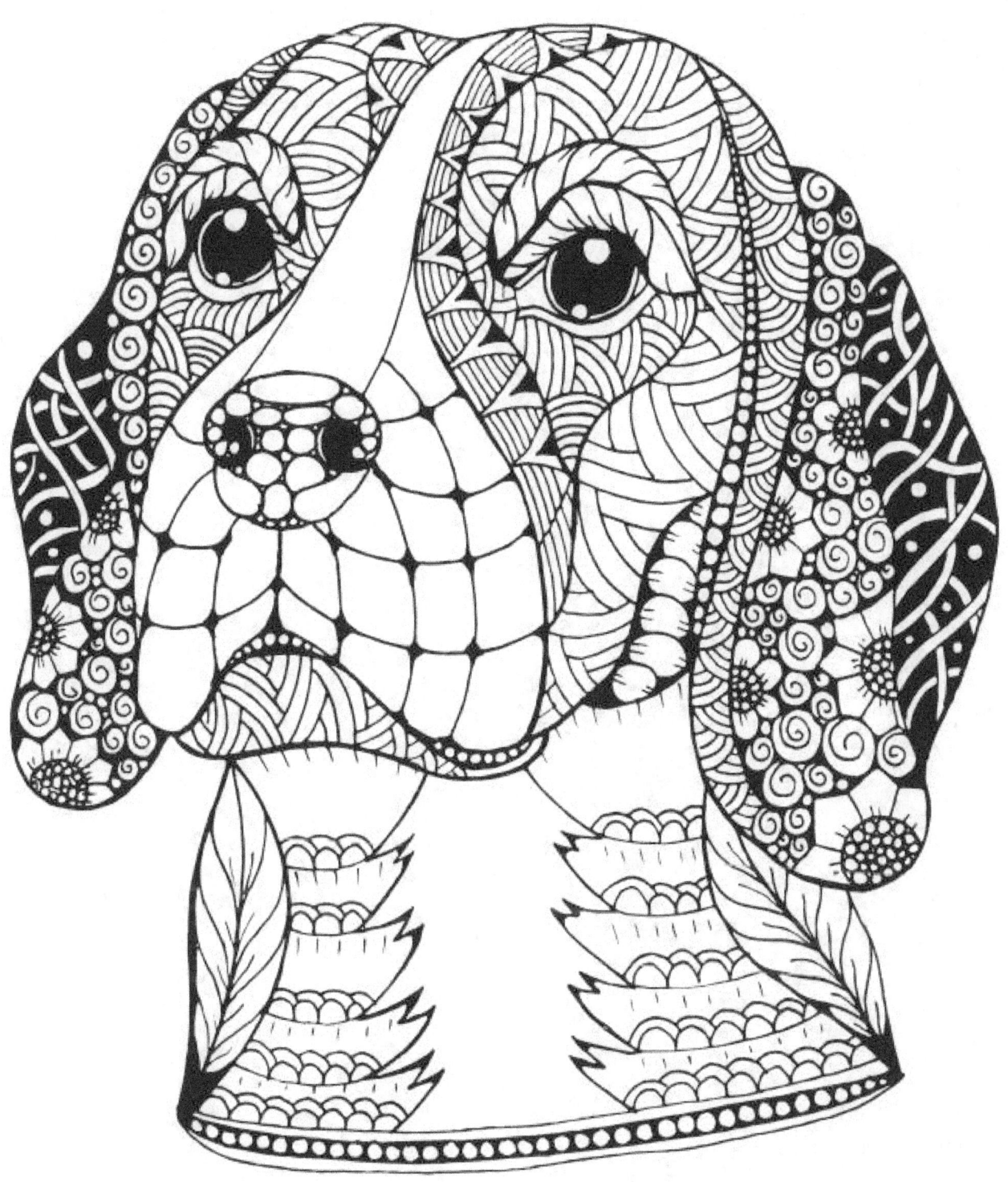

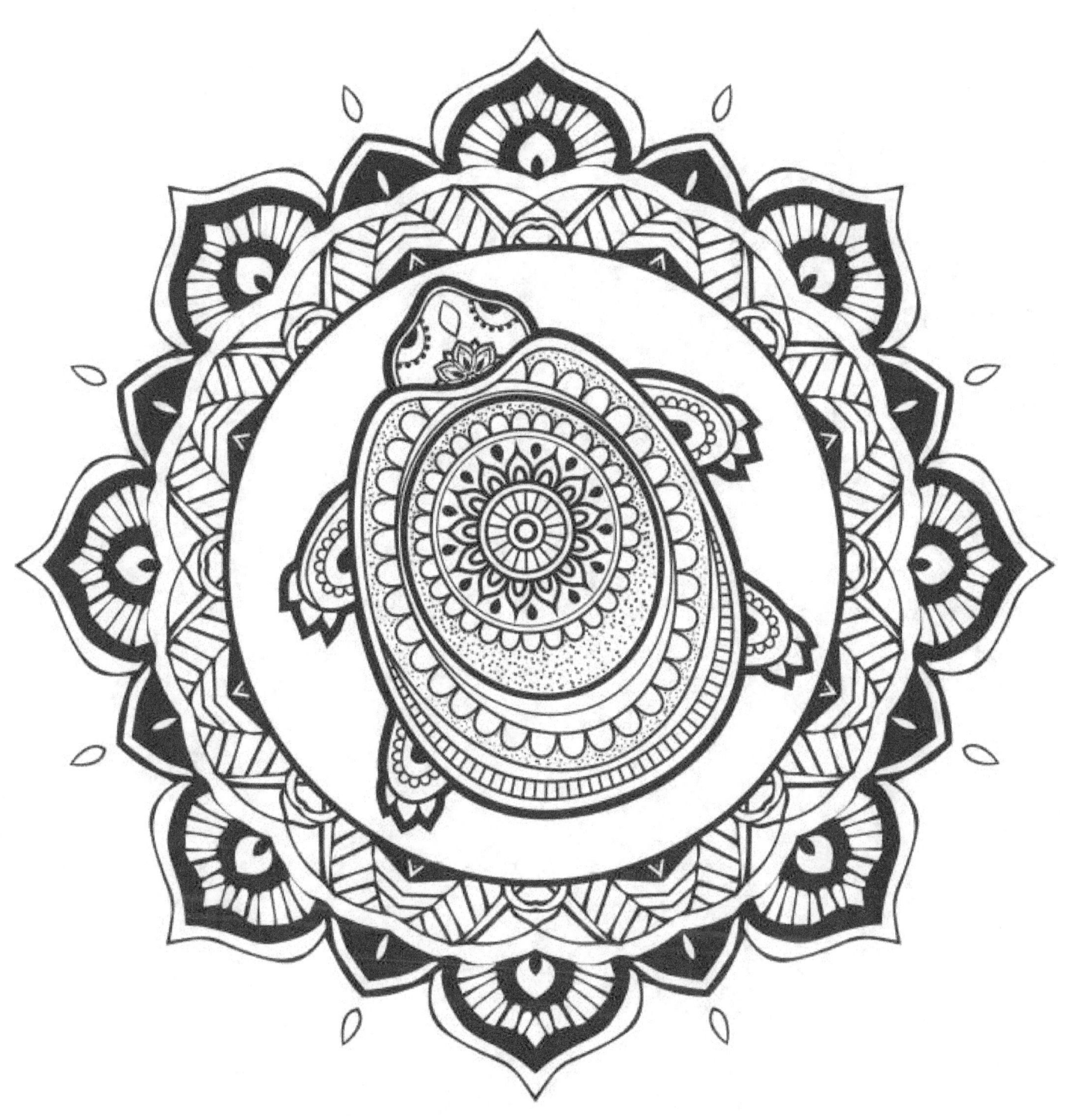

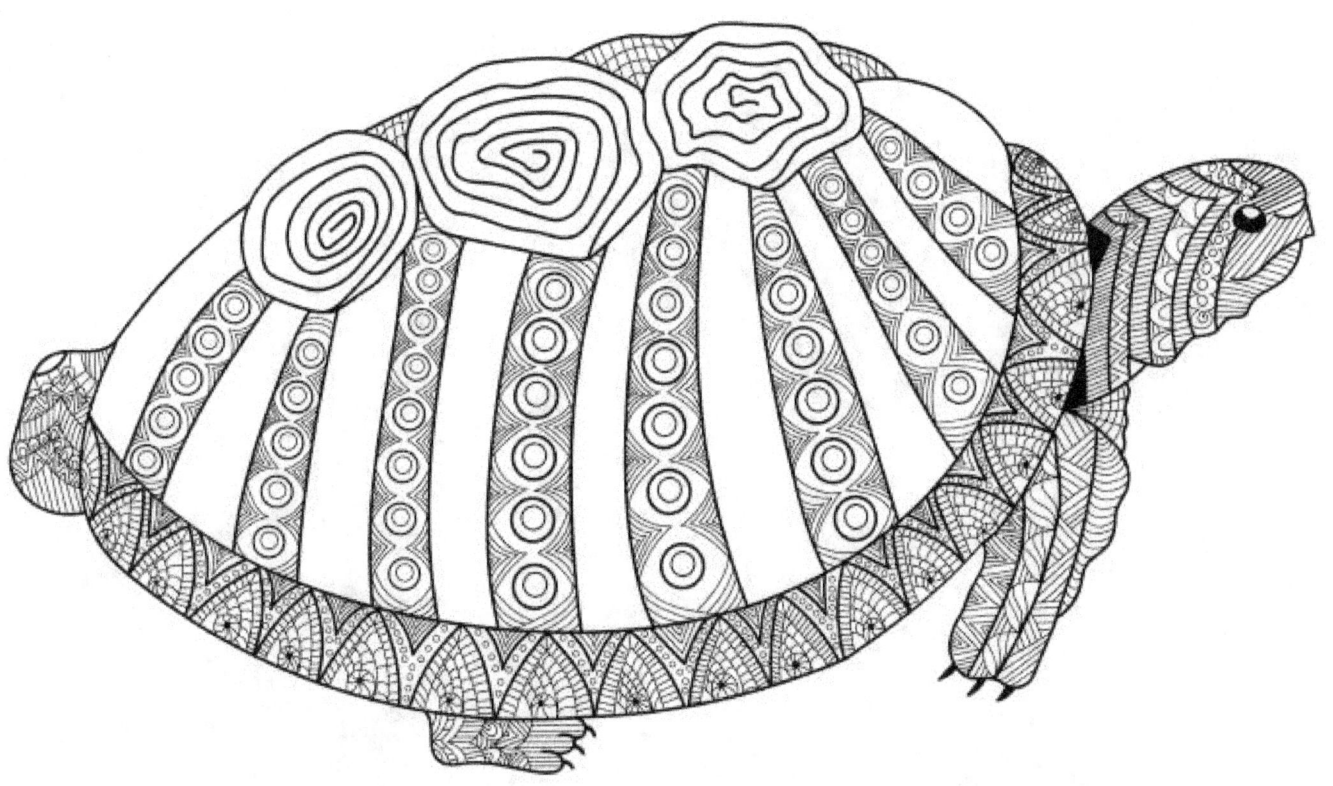

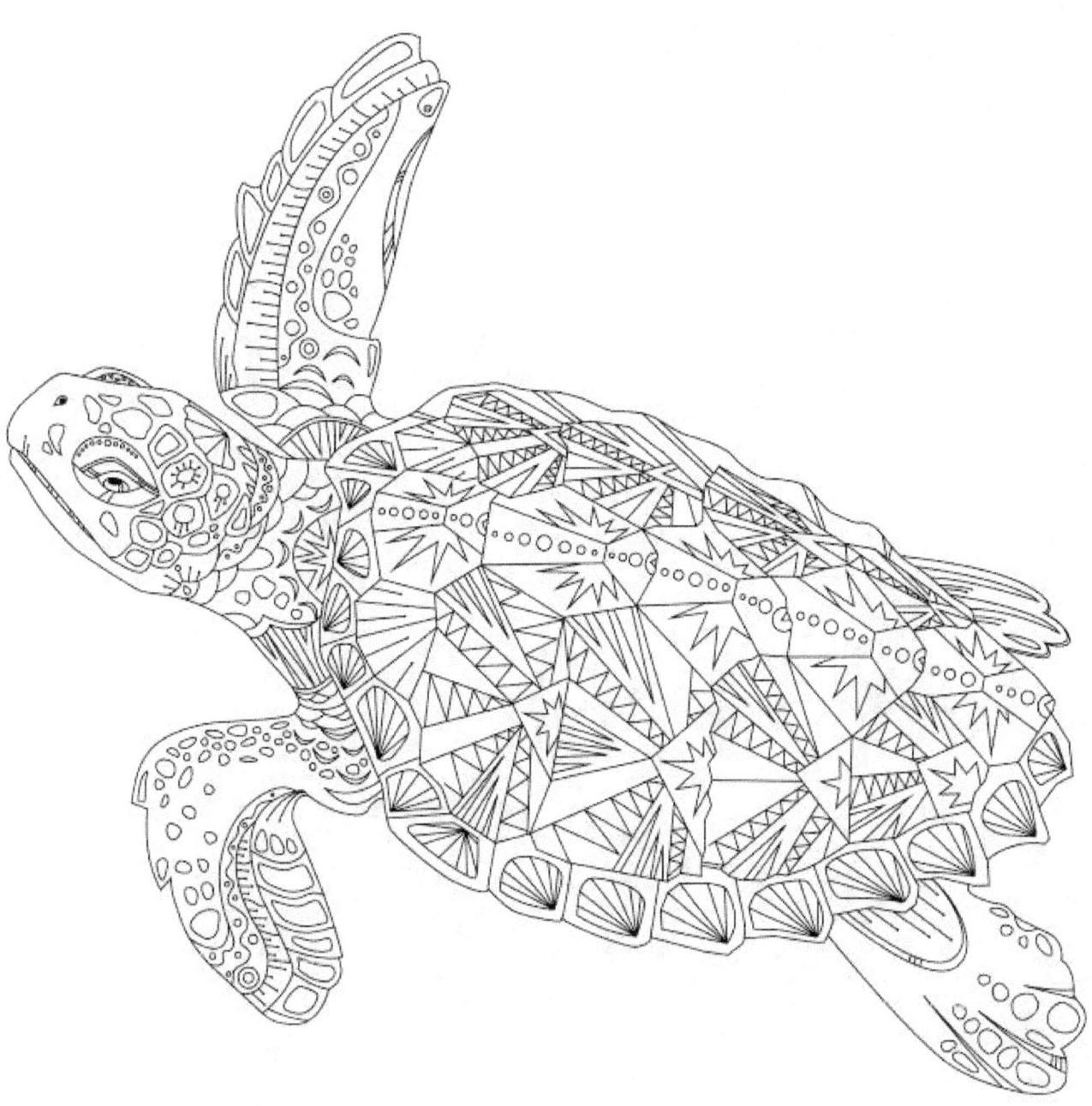

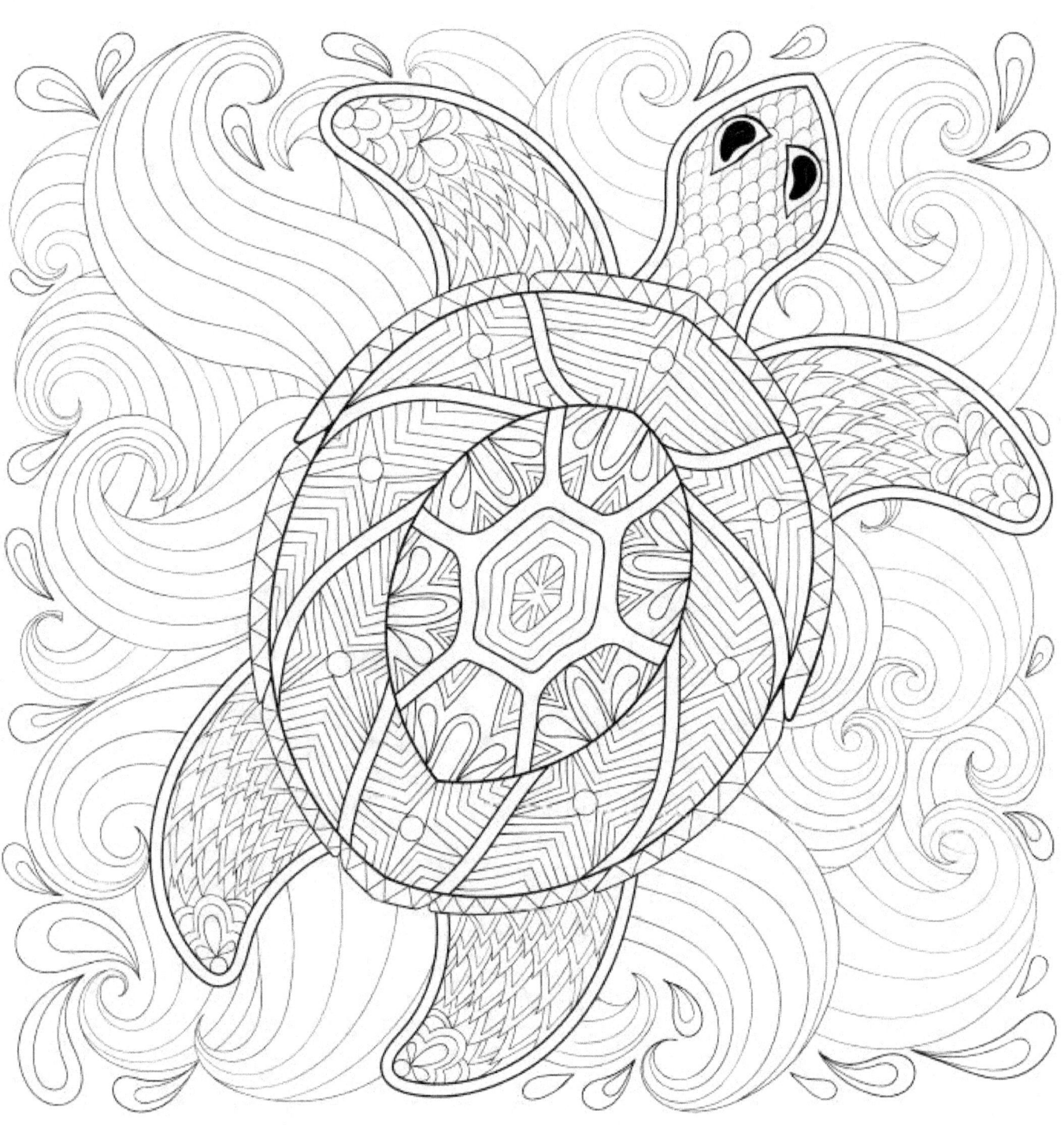

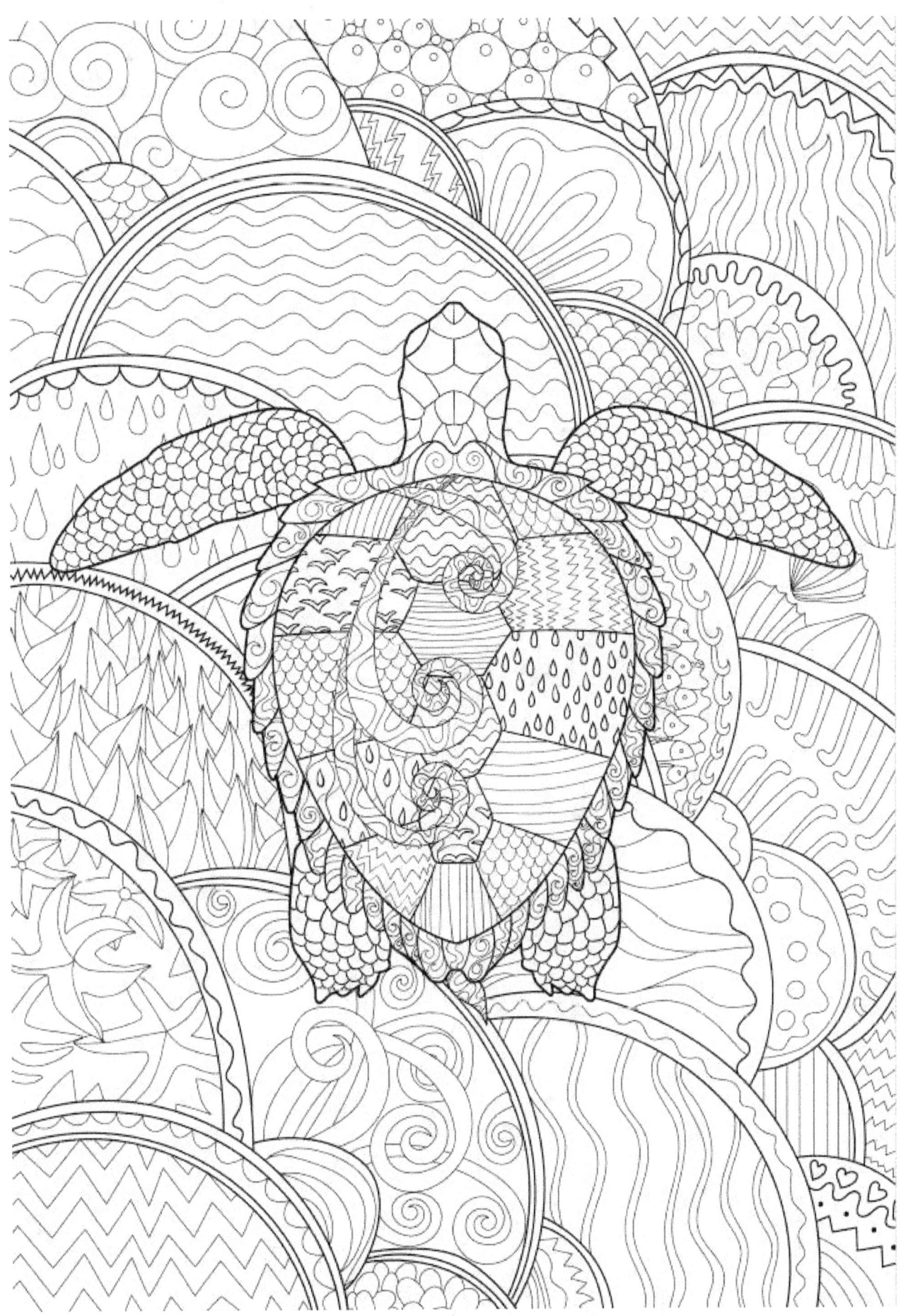

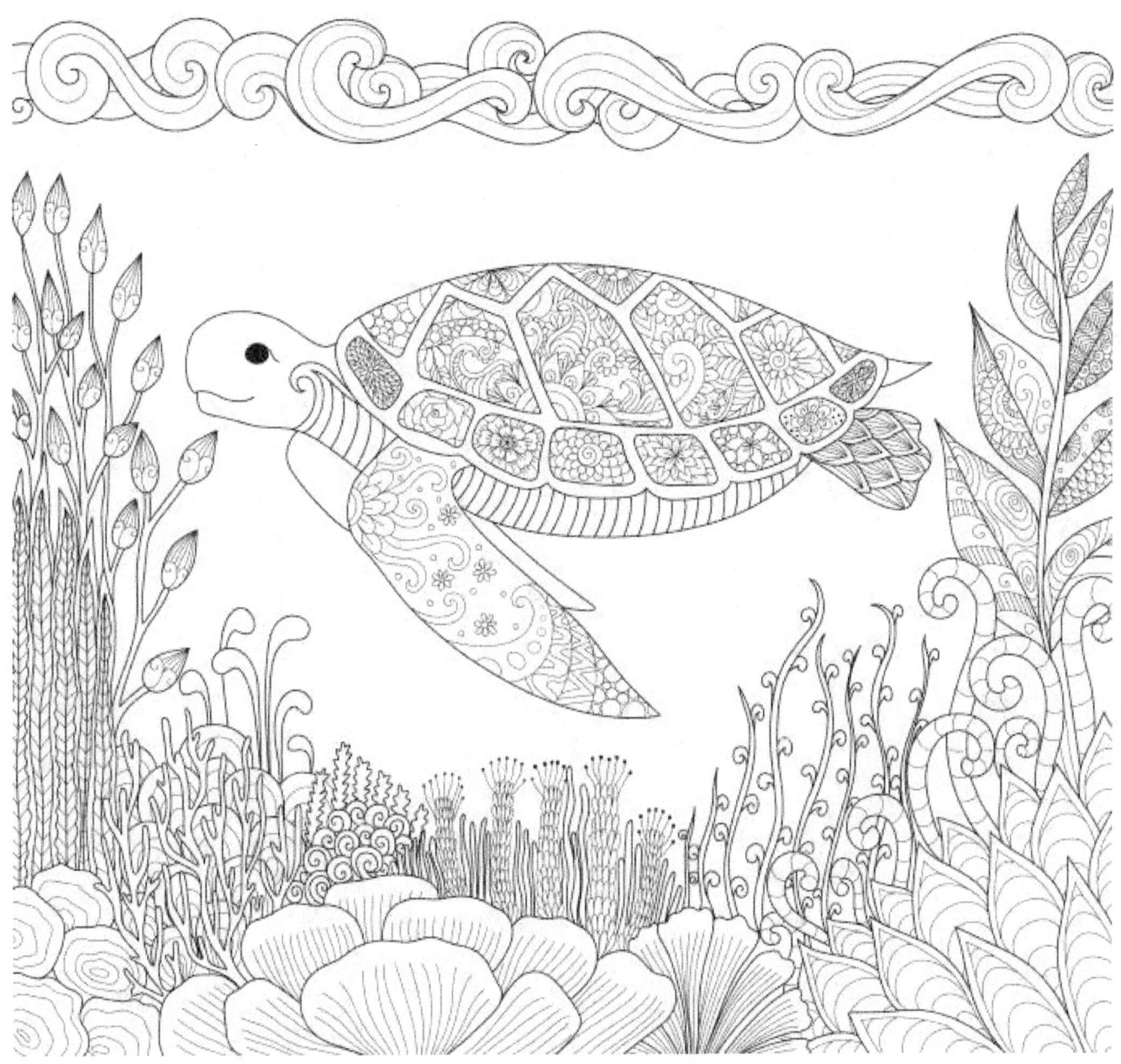

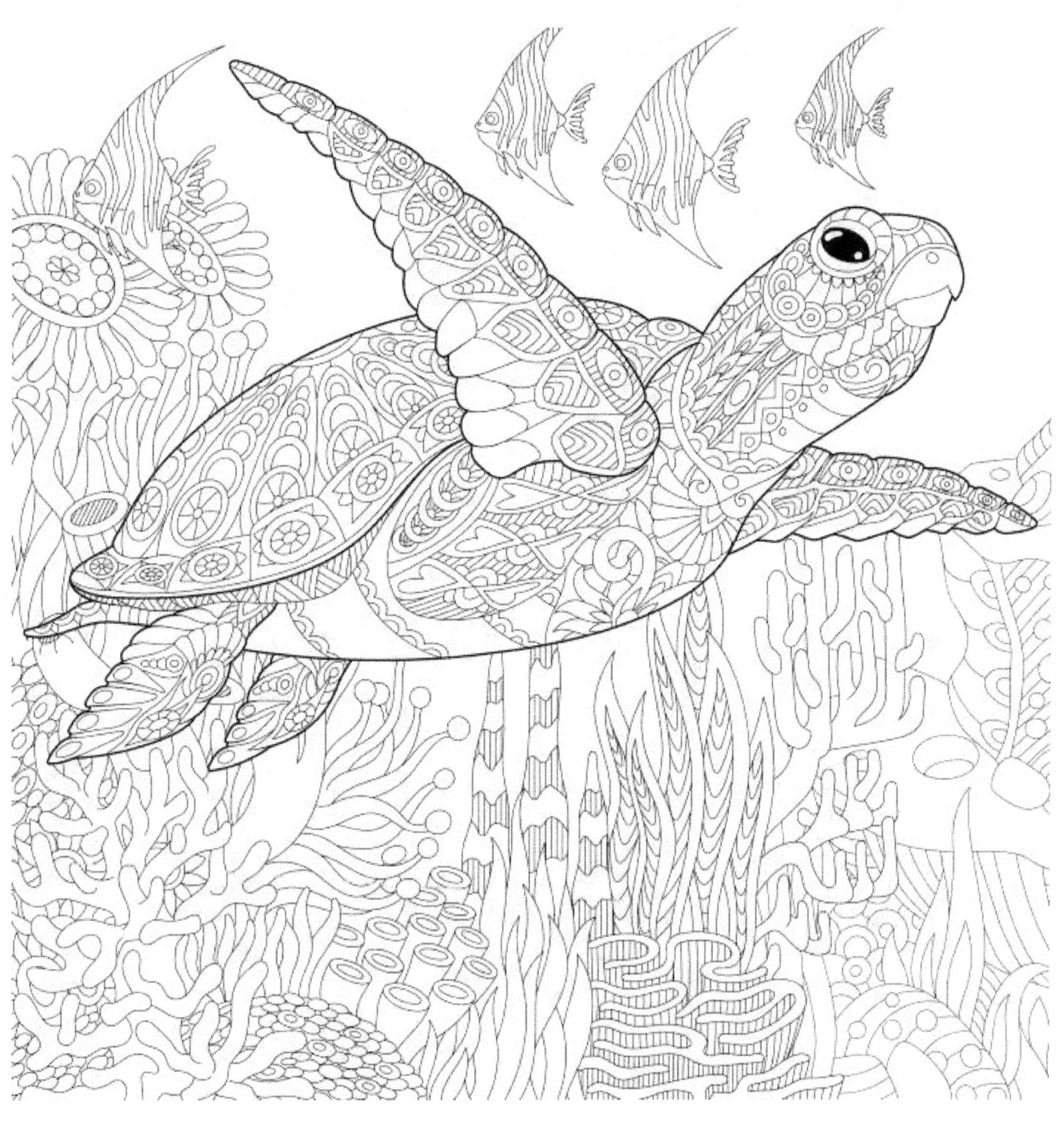

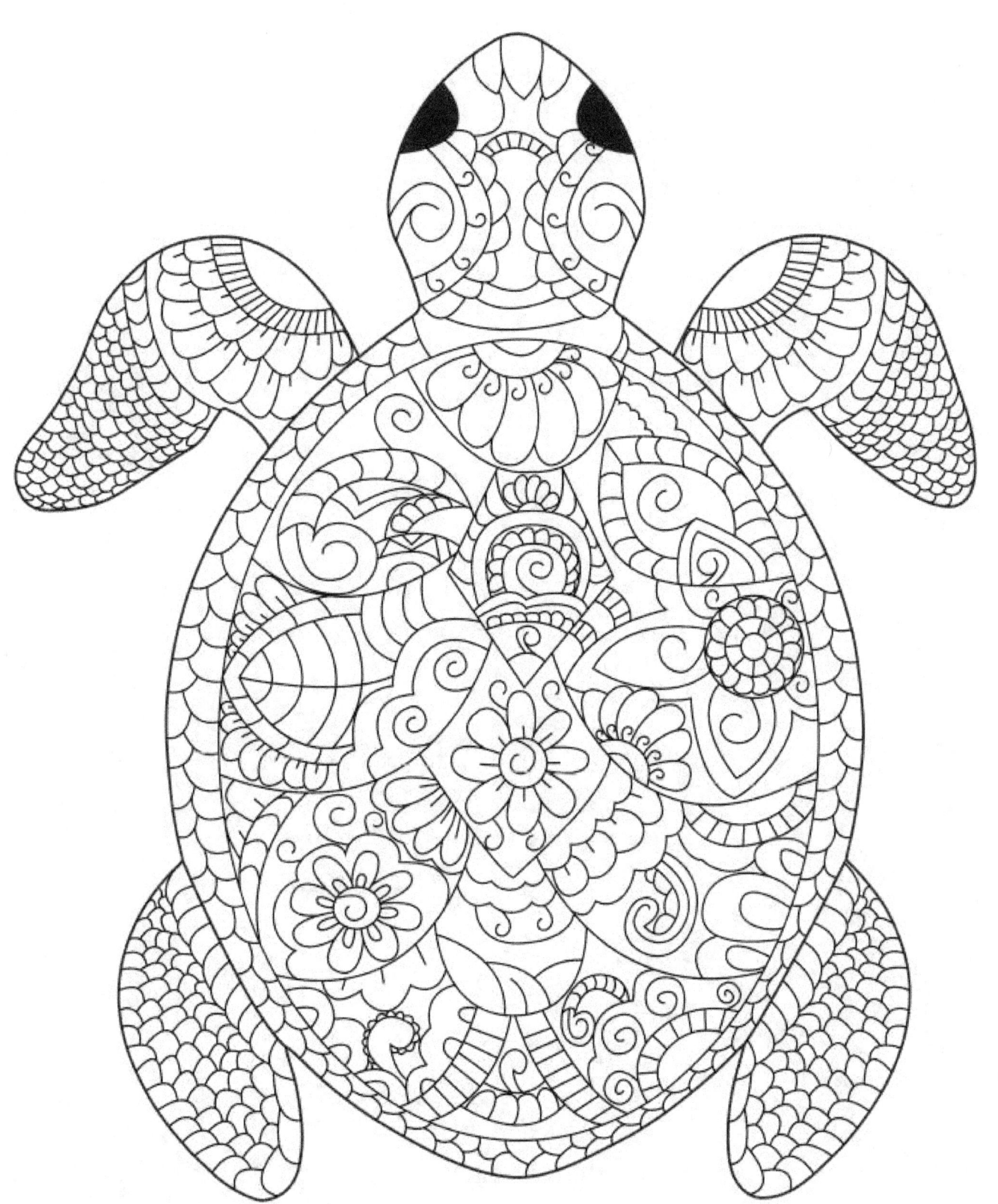

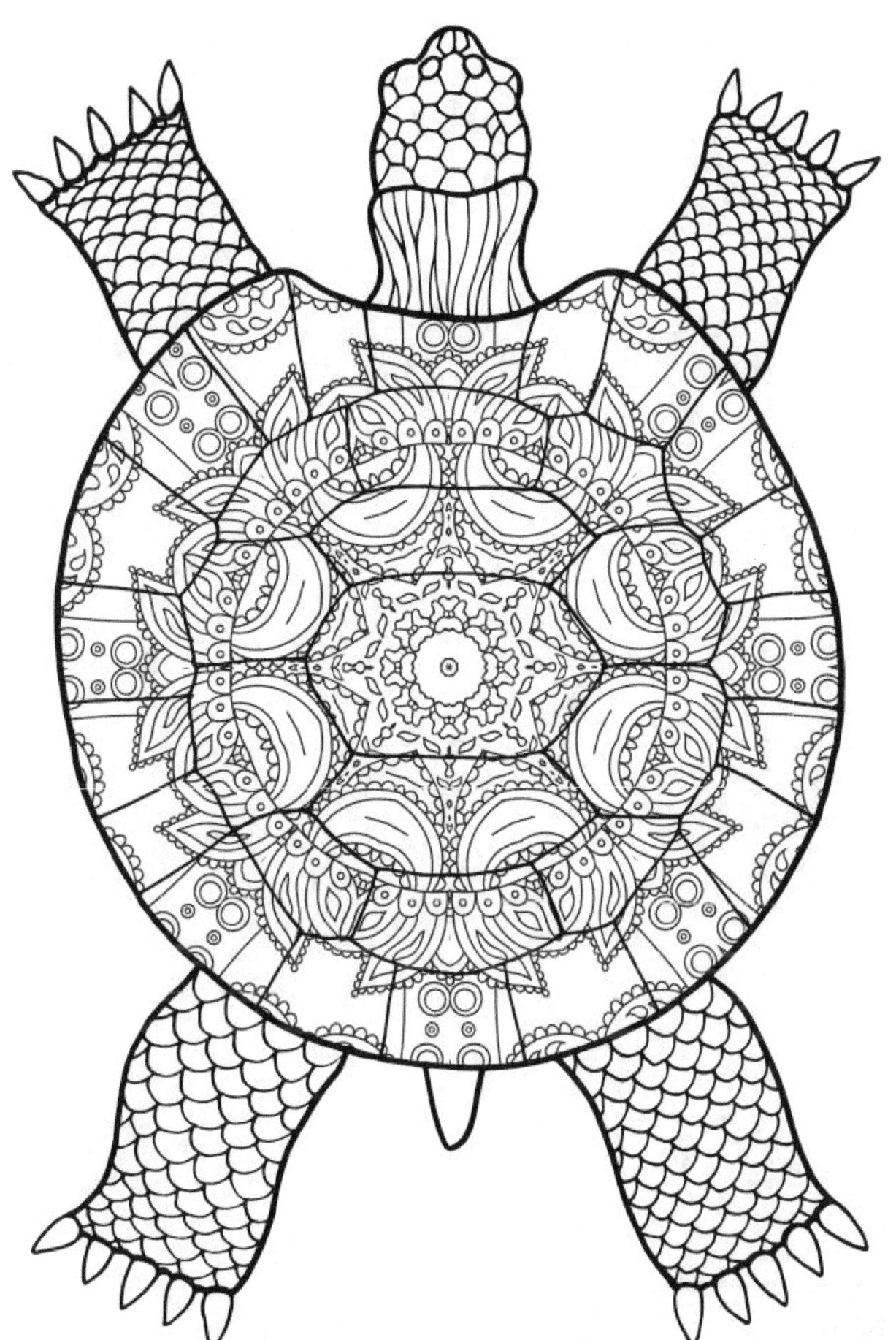

www.ingramcontent.com/pod-product-compliance
Lightning Source LLC
Chambersburg PA
CBHW081217170526
45165CB00009B/2852